GREECE IN THE 1940S

DIGITAL ACTIVISM AND SOCIETY: POLITICS, ECONOMY AND CULTURE IN NETWORK COMMUNICATION

The *Digital Activism and Society: Politics, Economy and Culture in Network Communication* series focuses on the political use of digital everyday-networked media by corporations, governments, international organizations (Digital Politics), as well as civil society actors, NGOs, activists, social movements and dissidents (Digital Activism) attempting to recruit, organize and fund their operations, through information communication technologies.

The series publishes books on theories and empirical case studies of digital politics and activism in the specific context of communication networks. Topics covered by the series include, but are not limited to:

- the different theoretical and analytical approaches of political communication in digital networks;
- studies of sociopolitical media movements and activism (and 'hacktivism');
- transformations of older topics such as inequality, gender, class, power, identity and group belonging;
- strengths and vulnerabilities of social networks.

Series Editor

Dr Athina Karatzogianni

About the Series Editor

Dr Athina Karatzogianni is an Associate Professor at the University of Leicester, UK. Her research focuses on the intersections between digital media theory and political economy, in order to study the use of digital technologies by new sociopolitical formations.

Published Books in This Series

Digital Materialism: Origins, Philosophies, Prospects by Baruch Gottlieb

Nirbhaya, New Media and Digital Gender Activism by Adrija Dey

Digital Life on Instagram: New Social Communication of Photography by Elisa Serafinelli

Internet Oligopoly: The Corporate Takeover of Our Digital World by Nikos Smyrnaios

Digital Activism and Cyberconflicts in Nigeria: Occupy Nigeria, Boko Haram and MEND by Shola A. Olabode

Platform Economics: Rhetoric and Reality in the "Sharing Economy" by Cristiano Codagnone

Communication as Gesture: Media(tion), Meaning, & Movement by Michael Schandorf

Digital Media and the Greek Crisis: Cyberconflicts, Discourses and Networks by Ioanna Ferra and Athina Karatzogianni

Journalism and Austerity: Digitization and Crisis During the Greek Memoranda by Christos Kostopoulos

The Emerald Handbook of Digital Media in Greece: Journalism and Political Communication in Times of Crisis by Anastasia Veneti and Athina Karatzogianni

Protest Technologies and Media Revolutions by Athina Karatzogianni, Michael Schandorf and Ioanna Ferra

Posthumanism in Digital Culture: Cyborgs, Gods and Fandom by Callum T. F. McMillan

Chinese Social Media: Face, Sociality, and Civility by Shuhan Chen and Peter Lunt

Posthumanism in Digital Culture: Cyborgs, Gods and Fandom by Callum T. F. McMillan

Media, Technology and Education in a Post-Truth Society: From Fake News, Datafication and Mass Surveillance to the Death of Trust by Alex Grech

3D Printing Cultures, Politics and Hackerspaces by Leandros Savvides

Environmental Security in Greece: Perceptions From Industry, Government, NGOs and the Public by Charis(Harris) Gerosideris

Fantasy, Neoliberalism and Precariousness: Coping Strategies in the Cultural Industries by Jérémy Vachet

Crisis Communication in China: Strategies Taken by the Chinese Government and Online Public Opinion by Wei Cui

Digital Politics, Digital Histories, Digital Futures: New Approaches for Historicising, Politicising and Imagining the Digital by Adi Kuntsman and Liu Xin

Digital Memory in Brazil: A Fragmented and Elastic Negationist Remembrance of the Dictatorship by Leda Balbino

Duty to Revolt: Transnational and Commemorative Aspects of Revolution by George Souvlis and Athina Karatzogianni

Organisation and Governance Using Algorithms by Ioannis Avramopoulos

Fractal Leadership by Athina Karatzogianni and Jacob Matthews

Future Feminisms: Biolabour, Technofeminist Care, and Transnational Strategies by Ioanna Ferra, Fenia Ferra, Korinna Patelis and Athina Karatzogianni

Forthcoming Titles

Platform Governance and Social Justice by Paloma Viejo Otero

Massively Marginal: Kuaishou as China's Subaltern Platform by Dino Ge Zhang, Jian Xu and Gabriele de Seta

Visual Misogyny: Platformed Politics of Visual Gendered Hate by Patricia Prieto-Blanco and Suay Melisa Özkula

Untangling Platform Power: The Oppositional Affordances of Data Activism by Venetia Papa

Massively Marginal: Kuaishou as China's Subaltern Platform by Dino Ge Zhang, Jian Xu, and Gabriele de Seta

The Road to Neo-Feudalism: Syriza, Melancholy and the Future by Korinna Patelis

GREECE IN THE 1940S: OCCUPATION AND CIVIL WAR IN DIGITAL CULTURE, SCREEN MEDIA, AND THE ARTS

EDITED BY

LEANDROS SAVVIDES
University of Cyprus, Cyprus

AND

IOANNA FERRA
HSE University, Russia

United Kingdom – North America – Japan – India
Malaysia – China

Emerald Publishing Limited
Emerald Publishing, Floor 5, Northspring, 21-23 Wellington Street, Leeds LS1 4DL

First edition 2025

Editorial matter and selection © 2025 Ioanna Ferra and Leandros Savvides.
Individual chapters © 2025 The authors.
Published under exclusive licence by Emerald Publishing Limited.

Reprints and permissions service
Contact: www.copyright.com

No part of this book may be reproduced, stored in a retrieval system, transmitted in any form or by any means electronic, mechanical, photocopying, recording or otherwise without either the prior written permission of the publisher or a licence permitting restricted copying issued in the UK by The Copyright Licensing Agency and in the USA by The Copyright Clearance Center. Any opinions expressed in the chapters are those of the authors. Whilst Emerald makes every effort to ensure the quality and accuracy of its content, Emerald makes no representation implied or otherwise, as to the chapters' suitability and application and disclaims any warranties, express or implied, to their use.

British Library Cataloguing in Publication Data
A catalogue record for this book is available from the British Library

ISBN: 978-1-83753-647-4 (Print)
ISBN: 978-1-83753-646-7 (Online)
ISBN: 978-1-83753-648-1 (Epub)

INVESTOR IN PEOPLE

CONTENTS

1. The Greek 1940s: Constructing Collective Memory in Digital Culture, Screen Media, and the Arts 1
   Leandros Savvides and Ioanna Ferra

2. A "Civil War" That Has No End: Historical Revisionism and Politics (Ένας «εμφύλιος» που δεν παρέρχεται: ιστορικός αναθεωρητισμός και πολιτική) 11
   Yannis Skalidakis

3. The Greek Civil War in Film 25
   Panagiotis Dendramis

4. This War will be Either Televised or Taped: WWII in the Greek Domestic Entertainment Until the Deregulation (1971–1989) 43
   Ursula-Helen Kassaveti

5. German Conquerors in the Greek Full-Length Fiction Films From 1945 to 1981 63
   Yiorgos Andritsos

6. "Other" Debts: The German WWII Debt to Greece in the German Press and "The Greek Crisis" Context 81
   Yiannis Mylonas

7. Misrepresentation or Justification? The Politics of Greek Civil War Memory Through the Case of a Palimpsest Memorial 107
   Theodoros Kouros

8. Digitally Mediated Collective Memory of the Greek Civil War: A Post-Memory Analysis of YouTube Comments 129
   Leandros Savvides and Ioanna Ferra

1

THE GREEK 1940S: CONSTRUCTING COLLECTIVE MEMORY IN DIGITAL CULTURE, SCREEN MEDIA, AND THE ARTS

LEANDROS SAVVIDES[a] AND IOANNA FERRA[b]

[a]University of Cyprus, Cyprus
[b]HSE University, Russia

Keywords: Collective memory; media studies; ideological hegemony; digital culture; politics of memory

There has been a prolonged and diffused discussion about the nature and the purpose of defining history, in the context of "the end of history" (Fukuyama, 1992). Indeed, contemporary scholars operate within a rich intellectual landscape of complex debates, as this emerged by the intersections of memory studies and cultural production. These intense debates around the conceptualization of memory/memory construction, history, and culture illustrate how individuals and societies engage with and interpret the past (Erll & Nünning, 2008; Radstone, 2020; Tamm, 2013). In this context, technology had a significant impact in shaping the relationship between memory and historical experience, as well as memory and political identities. This new complexity dominated by a shift in the process of interpreting history, redetermining the hegemonic forces and crafting historical narratives. At the same time, this shift challenged the prevailing certainties which established over the past three decades, following the collapse of the Soviet Union, contributing to the transition from a unipolar world to a multipolar one. In this destabilized context, examples of historical revisionism are either consciously pursued or resulted as part of cultural markets. Such examples indicate the value and impact of mobilizing a variety of narratives, modalities, formats, and mediums in order to reconsider the past and interpret history. In the case of Greece, some of these points can be observed within the doctrine of alleviating the political discourse and historical narratives from the "ideological hegemony of the left."

Mylonas (2024) notes that there is a growing interest by citizen initiatives to embark on interventions in the public sphere, offering counternarratives of history. Such endeavors could be associated with the concern of losing a cultural aspect of collective memory that was once widespread. These initiatives are more likely to push the boundaries of the increasingly shrinking public sphere to form political subjectivities, as mass politics have been in crises and in constant decrease in legitimacy since the retreat from class (Wood, 1998), discrediting for grand narratives of the world at the expense of managerial and technocratic responses to politics. What seems to be the pattern is that historical revisionism is a constant battle between social, political, and economic forces. Memory and collective memory (one that can take the form of cultural signifier) of large groups of people appear to be a powerful tool that political actants are trying to shape for political ends, as they become of primary importance for shaping political identities of the future.

The new multipolar world seems to have no reference point, everything is in flux. Different examples and events, including regional wars, indicate a challenge regarding reading and building histories, situating these are "in the right side of history." The Russian–Ukrainian conflict is a great example regarding building narration and memory, pointing out historical continuities. In only some of the dominant frames, this conflict became known as a "Special Operation" in Russia's narration or, in a different approach, a war between the Western powers and the United States, with proxy the Ukrainian government and Russia, making in both cases strong references around the rise and the defeat of Nazism in the World War II (WWII). While this seems like a refraction of what is at stake, there is a brewing discussion on whether history is indeed again on the move, as competing powers pose no alternative to each other.

Notably, this is not the first time that historical continuities are constructed and debated during periods of recent crises and political turmoil, with reference to WWII. In the European context, similar examples can be found on different occasions, with some of the most indicative coming from the global recessions and the anti-austerity movement. The ideological and political turmoil of the interwar and WWII period looked both on the division between the European North vs South, as well as on the ideological differences and the rise of far-right politics, populism, etc., while at the same time, questions around class, poverty, and inequality formulated drawing from historical continuities and debates, as shaped after WWII.

This is where the politics of memory becomes significant. The intensity by which each political force manufactures their own narrative gives an insight into the way that contemporary disputes emerge. To this end, each political actant has now a wealth of mediums that they can use to construct narratives and distribute them within multiple societies. While classic 20th century ways of narrative construction could take the route of institutional infrastructure, funding agencies, large scale cultural projects such as films, or systematic media coverage of news from a certain angle, the development of digital media, and the proliferation of cultural products online, alongside the engagement of users, provide another terrain in which the politics of memory take place.

Looking at the case of Greece, the so-called and heavily projected Greek Crisis and the anti-austerity movement, the political turmoil and polarization of those days reflected in the rise of far right, bringing under (re) consideration and in the public discourse some of the most significant periods of the contemporary history of the country, including Occupation and Civil War. At the same time, during the last decades, there were several films and documentaries concentrating on that period, while in the digital sphere, there are often references and debates which highlight the historical continuities, starting since the 1940s.

In the literature, there are several studies focusing on the representation of Occupation and Civil War, and more recently, expanding the discussion to the construction of collective memory. Therefore, digital media indicated another aspect regarding the way that the turmoiled decade of 1940s is seen in contemporary media. The emergence of digital media, either in the form of social media and algorithmic curation, or in the field of digitization of news focusing more on journalism, puts into the spotlight questions regarding digital collective memory and historical continuities. This book aims to contribute to the field by offering scholarly insights into an emerging field. It examines how various forms of media, particularly within the evolving cultural industry and digitization, shape the construction of collective memory regarding the 1940s. The book focuses on further expanding the discussion regarding media contribution in shaping collective memory, as similar patterns can be seen in different countries, integrating the debate within interdisciplinary frames of culture, science and technology studies (STS), and media studies. Starting with Yiannis Skalidakis' chapter, which traces the roots of conscious historical revisionism strategies in Greece, this edited volume expands the discussion beyond history per se. It focuses more on how history is constructed, produced, and consumed within the landscape of different media and audiences. The book concentrated on the evolution of technology and the transition to the digital media context, which brought new and old questions regarding memory construction and the media, under consideration.

Thus, this edited volume provides an insight into the Greek 1940s, as seen in different forms of media, exploring the construction of collective memory and concentrating on some of the most significant historical sequence of events of the contemporary Greek history (Occupation, Civil War, etc.). These sequences of military and political turning points are important as they can draw important conclusions about winners and defeated of the war and the political implications for today's Greek political landscape. Some of these events, such as the brutal violence of the Nazi occupation in Greece, became an important cultural signifier during the last decade of memorandums and has been used by politicians to argue about the German–Greek relations during the Greek crisis and especially around the Greek Referendum, in 2015. Another important on which the book looks at is the Treaty of Varkiza in which the Resistance fighters, despite holding power in extensive territories immediately after the Occupation, have signified the withdrawal from a revolution and the focus on liberal democratic elections. The agreement (or treaty as is also known) effectively disarmed the faction predominantly credited with the liberation of Greece from Nazi occupation, rendering it impotent against a resurgent Greek state employing a military approach against the Resistance fighters. This has also left deep scars in Greek society, the cultural residue of which could be seen during the last decades of memorandums. Consequently, we believe that the field is not saturated of works; on the contrary, new mediums and developments suggest a resurgence on how collective memory is manipulated according to contemporary politics.

The 1940s is naturally considered as "a decade of social disintegration, political collapse, and mass violence unprecedented in degree and scale" (Mazower, 2000, p. 1). Greece experienced some of the most significant moments in its contemporary history which, as we shall see in the chapters, define the sociopolitical context even today. The postwar era was dominated by right-wing narratives which had a significant impact on the development of collective (historical) memory, as seen in different countries. In Greece, the dominant narrative surrounding the Occupation and Civil War has been shaped by the historical changes and democratic struggles that followed. This evolution spans from the 1960s, with discussions of sociopolitical resistance, to the extreme right-wing discourse of the military dictatorship in the 1970s, and eventually to the "political reconciliation" of the 1980s. This reconciliation marked the beginning of a new historical era in which the political system fostered a sense of national polarization and disunity (*dichonia*).

Up until the late 1980s, literature largely focused on the resistance during the Occupation. However, from the early 1990s onward, scholarly attention expanded to include topics such as the Civil War and collaboration with the Axis.

Even though lately, there has been an increased focus on the investigation of this period, it is the dominant media industries which constructed in different ways the public discourse and collective memory of the Civil War to this day. On the other hand, latest approaches on the study of Occupation and Civil War suggest that the media silencing of the forces of liberation is followed by an intensified academic attempt at the rewriting of history. Conservative academic historians drive this process, claiming a sort of "hegemony of the left," "myths and violence of the left" in public discourse, which was developed especially after the fall of the military junta in 1974. Historians such as Nikos Marantzidis (2013) and Stathis Kalyvas (2006) suggest that left-wing forces are unjustified to assert that their efforts are not being represented enough or proportionally in media and official historiography.

On the contrary, there is a suggestion that the violence perpetrated by the Resistance forces is what resulted in the brutal occupation practices applied by the Nazis, explaining the Civil War/post-Civil War state emergence and practice of persecution of communists, socialists, democrats, or sympathizers. Rewriting history, along so-called objective lines, shows that the claims of the left regarding the historiographic representation are untrue and therefore illegitimate. As Skalidakis describes in his chapter, such "objective lines" are based on futile attempts to describe their agendas as objective research. Latest studies show that such an attempt by historians fits into a framework of liberal democratic Europe, thus having a specific ideological agenda, which in no way holds an objective outlook on history. In other words, such frameworks of analyzing and rewriting history fit into the description of a continuation of the Civil War in other ways because such revision of history is producing and reproducing ideology, politics, and power by scholarly means.

Considering the impact of the 1940s on influencing and polarizing Greek political culture to this day, this edited volume brings together academics, researchers, and practitioners to investigate the historical continuities and discontinuities in the public discourse and the creation of diverse sets of publics, polarization and conflict in Greece, and internationally. At the same time, this book focuses on how different forms of media contribute to the construction of public discourse and collective memory online and offline, as observed focusing on different forms of media – from films to journalism, to art and digital media. Finally, the book attempts to bring into attention the connection between traditional and interdisciplinary approaches, pointing out the continuity of traditional historical revisionist mediums and attempts and the use of new digital/computational methods, for studying contemporary media contribution and practices, regarding the representation of the 1940s.

As a way to develop an insight into what that forms the backdrop and basis upon which politics of memory take place, the book starts by introducing some key debates around historical revisionism and the Civil War. In the second chapter, Yannis Skalidakis discusses contemporary approaches regarding the "Wars of Memory" and the way that WWII is conceptualized and memorized nowadays. What is the impact in contemporary politics? Skalidakis argues that while Kalyvas and Marantzidis present their work as a scientific endeavor, their revisionist approach is driven by a predetermined political agenda. Their emphasis lies in condemning the left as a totalitarian or even criminal force, rather than genuinely re-evaluating historical interpretations.

One aspect of their revisionist project involves documenting leftist violence during the Nazi occupation period, portraying it as a precursor to the broader narrative of the Greek Civil War. This perspective overlooks the historical context of the occupation and employs selective methods of data collection, such as body counting, to support their claims. Skalidakis draws parallels between Kalyvas and Marantzidis' approach and that of the German New Right, highlighting their attempts to discredit alternative historical interpretations and portray themselves as victims of ideological suppression. Ultimately, the overarching goal of historical revisionism in Greece, as in other contexts, is to denigrate and marginalize leftist ideologies and resistance movements, thereby shaping the political landscape of the present.

Then, Panagiotis Dendramis discusses the Greek Civil War, as seen in films. The author concentrates on the way that the conflict between the opposite sites, the Hellenic Army (ΕΣ) and the Democratic Army (ΔΣ), produced and reproduced in cinema pointing on the peculiar dialectic relationship between history and cinema. As he points, history and cinema are in constant interaction. Movies represent human stories, which have a significant impact on the way we contract past remembrance. The author illustrated key factors that influence the creation of films, including artistic vision and motives. Focusing on the dialectic relationship between history and cinema, starting from the period of conflict, this relationship was later undermined for two decades reflecting on the formation of new sociopolitical structures. Then, this discussion around cinema and history, re-evolved during the 1970s, having particular artistic and ideological characteristics, and since re-emerges from time to time capturing public attention.

Focusing on traditional media, the next chapter by Ursula-Helen Kassaveti delves deeper into representations of WWII, not only in films but also within the broader Greek entertainment landscape. This analysis covers how these representations were shaped up until the era of audiovisual deregulation in the early 1990s. The term "audiovisual deregulation" refers to the process of relaxing or removing government regulations and restrictions aiming to promote competition, innovation, and investments in the media sector, raising though concerns regarding media concentration, cultural homogenization, and the quality of programming. By employing quantitative and qualitative approaches, the Kassaveti explores the question regarding how cultural products (e.g., Greek TV Series, etc.) echoed particular stances, historical continuities and discontinuities, within the pre-existing representations of War and Nation, as shaped within the realm of state television and domestic entertainment scene.

In Chapter 5 and 6, the focus moved to the representation of the "Others" both in films and journalism. Next, Yiorgos Andritsos explores further the association between films and the historical understanding of the 1940s, by concentrating on the way that the representation of the German conquerors evolved and transformed in films, from the mid-1940s up to the early 1980s. During the examined period, traditional media and especially films exert an enormous influence over the shaping of popular historical understanding. The author distinguished three key periods reflecting on significant sociopolitical development in Greece: from the end of Occupation to the imposing of the dictatorship, then the period during dictatorship up to the fall of junta, and finally the period up to Panhellenic Socialist Movement (PASOK) coming in power in the 1981 elections. The main queries that the author explored include issues over representation of German conquerors, the evolution over time, and aspects of the representation that remained constant within the examined period.

In Chapter 6, Yiannis Mylonas developed an insight into the ways in which Greece's war reparations discussed in the German news media. The author conducted a qualitative examination of 30 relevant articles sourced from the daily newspapers *FAZ* and *Die Welt*, spanning the period between 2015 and 2019, to delineate the predominant themes surrounding Greek reparations. Employing qualitative content analysis, coupled with insights from critical discourse analysis, the study scrutinized a corpus of 30 articles. While acknowledging the wartime atrocities perpetrated against Greece by the Wehrmacht and other occupying forces during WWII, the notion of debt as such is rebuffed, with Greek reparations demands being labeled as "populist" and "unattainable." Instead, a pragmatic and "forward-looking" approach is advocated, effectively implying a dismissal of the calls for war reparations.

The analysis concludes that divergent historical revisionist arguments inform the discourse within these newspapers, underscored by economic considerations and German nationalistic sentiments.

Theodoros Kouros, in Chapter 7, explored the construction of national narratives, as process of memory construction and impose to the community, and the community's response regarding this process. The dominant historical memory is closely associated to the notion of national identity, and these interdependent terms are dynamic and subject to transformations. This chapter focuses on these transformations by looking on what the author describes as "adventures" of the memorial and the way that these evolved during the second half of the 20th century, reflecting to the evolution of social memory and forgetting. Based on ethnographic field research ethnography, the study included observation of commemorations, interviews, as well as archival and bibliographical research, for developing an archaeology of the memorial. This study provides an insight into a case of alterations and neglect of memorializing materiality, alongside contestations related to the use of space, investigating the way that places of memory can reflect the evolving conception of the nation over time.

In the last chapter, we concentrated on digital media and the notion of digitally mediated collective memory. Drawing from the theoretical framework of post-memory (Hirsch, 2012), the study explores the significances of digital media, in shaping collective memory, via what appears to be a bottom-up process. We explored themes that emerged from users' engagement (comments) and contribution to the formation of public discourse. The aim was to make sense of this process as a site of politics of memory and open the discussion on reflecting what such sites of contention mean for the concept of public sphere and insert a seed of questioning form and content regarding the medium (Birkner & Donk, 2020; Hoskins, 2009).

The study explored YouTube as a platform that promotes social interaction, while at the same time shapes the discourse and frames among the digital online community. The analysis included more than 800 online comments of the most popular video regarding the Varkiza Treaty (view count/Synthiki tis Varkizas). The data were analyzed focusing on the production of mediated collective memory online and the articulation of a discussion regarding the affordances of digital media, in shaping the historical understanding and remembrance of the Greek Civil War. Starting from the notion of digitally mediated memory, as a form of post-memory, this chapter provides an insight into the context and the examined example, before situating it in the context of historical revisionism.

REFERENCES

Birkner, T., & Donk, A. (2020). Collective memory and social media: Fostering a new historical consciousness in the digital age? *Memory Studies*, *13*(4), 367–383.

Erll, A., & Nünning, A. A. (Eds.). (2008). *Cultural memory studies: An international and interdisciplinary handbook*. Walter de Gruyter.

Fukuyama, F. (1992). *The end of history and the last man*. The Free Press.

Hirsch, M. (2012). *The generation of postmemory: Writing and visual culture after the Holocaust*. Columbia University Press.

Hoskins, A. (2009). Digital network memory. In E. Erll & A. Rigney (Eds.), *Mediation, remediation, and the dynamics of cultural memory* (chapter 10). Walter de Gruyter.

Kalyvas, S. N. (2006). *The logic of violence in civil war*. Cambridge University Press.

Marantzidis, N. (2013). The Greek civil war (1944–1949) and the international communist system. *Journal of Cold War Studies*, *15*(4), 25–54.

Mazower, M. (2000). Changing trends in the historiography of postwar Europe, east and west. *International Labor and Working-Class History*, *52*, 275–282.

Mylonas, Y. (2024). Imperialism, revisionism, counter-hegemony, and the Greek 1940s as event. *Theory & Event*, *27*(1), 51–81.

Radstone, S. (2020). Working with memory: An introduction. In *Memory and methodology* (pp. 1–22). Routledge.

Tamm, M. (2013). Beyond history and memory: New perspectives in memory studies. *History Compass*, *11*(6), 458–473.

Wood, E. M. (1998). *The retreat from class: A new "true" socialism* (Rev. ed.). Verso.

2

A "CIVIL WAR" THAT HAS NO END: HISTORICAL REVISIONISM AND POLITICS
(Ένας «εμφύλιος» που δεν παρέρχεται: ιστορικός αναθεωρητισμός και πολιτική)

YANNIS SKALIDAKIS

University of Crete, Greece

Keywords: Wars of memory; historical revisionism; postcold war; Greek Civil War; revisionism as project

INTRODUCTION: AN UNFADING "CIVIL WAR": HISTORICAL REVISIONISM AND POLITICS

Seventy years following the conclusion of World War II (WWII) and the defeat of fascism, there are discernible indications that the discourse surrounding historical interpretations of the Second World War, or the "wars of memory," has taken a contentious trajectory. This is demonstrated by several events: firstly, on the 16th of March 2015, Latvia honored the Latvian Waffen SS Division, and concurrently, the Ukrainian parliament paid tribute to Roman Shukhevych, the former leader of an auxiliary unit, specifically Schutzmannschaft Battalion 201, which operated in Belarus during WWII. Shukhevych, notorious for his brutal actions against Jews and partisans, was an active collaborator with the Nazi regime. Additionally, the Ukrainian parliament extended homage to Petro Diachenko, commander of the 31st Schutzmannschafts Battalion SD in northwestern Ukraine, who played a leading role in mass atrocities committed against Jewish, Polish, and Ukrainian civilians and prisoners. Diachenko also participated in suppressing the Warsaw Uprising.

In Greece, the recollection of individuals who collaborated with Nazi occupiers remains predominantly subdued and self-censored (Κωστόπουλος, 2005). Nevertheless, a significant development emerged in 2015 when Stathis Kalyvas and Nikos Marantzidis released their impactful publication on the Greek Civil War, titled "Civil War Passions." This work underscored the necessity of dismantling the prevailing narrative related to the "German cholera," a narrative identified by the authors as integral to deconstructing the mythology associated with the left in Greece. In Hungary, President Viktor Orbán recently decried the "sovietisation" of Europe during the commemoration of the anti-communist uprising of 1956 (El País, 2023). Similarly, the Polish President, Andrzej Duda, expressed solidarity with his Hungarian counterpart and the Christian community in Hungary (President of Poland, 2023). These developments raise the question of whether, throughout history, the cause of suffering has perpetually revolved around the left, communism, and the former Soviet Union.

EUROPEAN CIVIL WAR

The momentous juncture in political and historiographical domains manifested itself unequivocally in 1989, marking the collapse of then existing socialist systems and the consequential transition to what can be characterized as the singular dominant global order, i.e., capitalism. Commencing in the 1990s, an extensive process of historiographical deconstruction and revision emerged, notably directed toward the examination of revolutionary events, ranging from the French Revolution to the Russian Revolution. This examination bore specific emphasis on the ideology of communism and its contentious characterization as a criminal phenomenon. During this revision process, the dreadful impediment posed by fascism, particularly Nazism, loomed large, given the indelible imprint of its genocidal policies epitomized by the Holocaust – the systematic extermination of Jews. This period witnessed a conscious attempt to establish comparative frameworks between communism and fascism/Nazism, encompassing their ideological underpinnings, governing systems, and broader sociopolitical structures. This endeavor sought to either establish communism as a more reprehensible system or indirectly assign blame for the crimes of fascism to the former. The overarching ideological counterpoint to both ideologies was the renewed liberal ideology, which characterized them as epitomes of "totalitarianism."

As articulated by the eminent historian Enzo Traverso in his work *History as a Battlefield* (2016), the prevailing zeitgeist at the inception of the 21st century is characterized by several defining elements. These include a strain of liberal anti-globalism, underpinned by a prevailing consensus in favor of humanism, and the pervasive naturalization of the prevailing societal order. Historians, operating within this contemporary sociopolitical milieu, find themselves situated amid these novel "epistemic" coordinates. It is paramount to acknowledge that the discipline of history invariably operates in tandem with the prevailing present, inextricably interwoven with the broader societal landscape.

Nonetheless, the contours of these developments, spanning from the tumultuous events of 1989 to the contemporary era, bear an unmistakable lineage with their origins traceable to the Cold War era. The interpretive framework that underpinned the anti-fascist struggle underwent a gradual process of deconstruction and reconstitution, ultimately culminating in the complex mosaic that characterizes the post-1989–1990 era. This transformation prompted the emergence of various manifestations and stages within the concurrent realms of political and historiographical revisionism. In light of these considerations, it is imperative to embark on a comprehensive exploration of the diverse expressions and temporal phases inherent to this dual trajectory of political and historical revisionism.

An increasingly pervasive interpretive framework for the initial half of the 20th century, which interconnects the occurrences of the two world wars – specifically those transpiring in the European context – with the interwar period, is the concept of the "European Civil War" that unfolded from 1914 to 1945, akin to a contemporary incarnation of the 30 Years' War. While this designation may appear paradoxical, the term "Civil War," when translated from Greek to English, does indeed denote a political war, shedding light on the essential nature of this interpretation. The schema commonly known as the "European Civil War" is an attempt to encapsulate a historical cycle in which the manifold contradictions that had been accumulating throughout the protracted phase of European capitalist ascendancy surfaced in a cataclysmic manner. These contradictions erupted vividly through the cataclysms of two world wars, and within this crucible, diverse ideological systems contended for supremacy during a pivotal period of historical transformation. Renowned historian Eric Hobsbawm characterizes the epoch between 1914 and 1945 as an international ideological Civil War, wherein Enlightenment principles (encompassing both the French and Russian Revolutions) clashed with their ideological antithesis, manifesting in the form of fascism (Hobsbawm, 2003).

However, the concept of the "European Civil War" took on a distinct interpretation in the book of the same title authored by the German historian Ernst Nolte in 1987. The comprehensive title of his work was "The European Civil War (1917–1945): National Socialism and Bolshevism" (Nolte, 2000). In this context, it is necessary to consider the matter of periodization, where the Civil War is not construed to have commenced in 1914 with the onset of World War I but rather in 1917, coinciding with the Bolshevik Revolution in Russia. Nolte posited that Bolshevism, in his view, arose from unjust circumstances, and National Socialism was framed as a response to these perceived injustices. The applicability of this framework to the Greek context will be elucidated below.

CONTROVERSY BETWEEN HISTORIANS AND BROADER IMPLICATIONS

The 1980s, marked by the conservative ideological wave championed by leaders like Ronald Reagan and Margaret Thatcher, bore witness to a momentous intellectual clash in West Germany, known as the Historikerstreit or historians' dispute. This dispute revolved around the fundamental nature of Nazism and the interpretation of the Holocaust, with its roots tracing back to an article authored by Ernst Nolte and published in the conservative daily, *Frankfurter Allgemeine Zeitung (FAZ)*, under the title "The Unfading Past." Nolte's contention was a provocative one; he asserted that the Nazi regime's "racial killings" could be construed as a defensive response to the Bolsheviks' "class killings." According to Nolte, the Soviet gulags held a position of primacy even in comparison to Auschwitz, and in this context, lending support to Hitler was, in his view, a rational German reaction to the perceived threat posed by Bolshevism. Nolte further contended that Hitler's eastward expansion was a legitimate act of self-defense against a genuinely imminent threat. These audacious revisionist perspectives set forth by Nolte elicited impassioned responses from other historians and intellectuals, perhaps most notably from the philosopher Jürgen Habermas. Concurrently, there were scholars who aligned with Nolte's efforts to relativize and, to a certain extent, justify German wartime atrocities and the broader Nazi regime. Paralleling this, a persistent effort sought to recalibrate the perception of Germany and the Germans from being viewed as the architects of the conflict to being framed as its victims.

In the course of his articles and interviews throughout the 1990s, Ernst Nolte began to articulate increasingly radical viewpoints. Notably, he voiced support for the perceived validity of specific Nazi policies and, astonishingly, identified a "rational core" within Nazi anti-Semitism. Moreover, in his biography of the philosopher Martin Heidegger, who had been a member of the Nazi party, Nolte asserted that National Socialism had represented the "correct path" for Germany in 1933 (Wolin, 2007).

In a remarkably insightful exploration of German revisionism, historian Richard Wolin, within his work "The Fascination of Irrationalism," established a connection between historical revisionism, right-wing political revisionism, and the emergence of a new right-wing political force in West Germany. This complex endeavor was rooted in the desire to relieve the collective sense of guilt regarding Germany's Nazi past and, concurrently, to shape a reinvigorated and assertive German identity. Remarkably, this period witnessed a resurgence of interest in the foremost figures of the conservative revolutionary movement in Germany during the 1920s, such as Carl Schmitt, Ernst Jünger, and Oswald Spengler. This resurgence marked a resurgence in intellectual interest, and topics associated with German national and cultural specificity – matters that had been marginalized due to their association with the Nazi ideology – were reintroduced into public discourse.

The strategy of this revisionist style, which starts from the historical past in order to influence the political present, is characteristic and shows striking similarities with what happened in Greece after a delay of some decades. The representatives of the new right programmatically proclaimed the goal of overthrowing the supposed ideological hegemony of the left and presented themselves as the "new generation" in opposition to the "old Left" of the 1960s. They were thus presented as "anti-establishment," as those who would tear down the taboos and orthodox statutes, the guardians of which were again the leftist historians. They did not fail to accuse the latter of regimentation and the silencing of freedom of speech and scientific debate.

In their attempt to restore German nationalism, they engaged in a revision of Nazism, relativizing (i.e., minimizing) its crimes and promoting its "positive" aspects, while at the same time, they systematically maximized the suffering suffered by the Germans in WWII, largely turning the perpetrators into victims. This new right was reinforced by the unification of the Germans and the de-glorification of German pride. Its influence reached the upper echelons of the ruling German right. One of its prominent spokesmen, the well-known Wolfgang Schäuble, did not hesitate to describe the German nation as a "community of protection and destiny" (Schütz-und Schicksalgemeinschaft), targeting the darker instincts of German patriotism, according to Wolin.

FROM RELATIVISM TO DENIAL

The relativization of Nazi crimes inevitably energized and stimulated a plethora of the most extreme views. The organized, systematic, and mass killing of between 5 and 6 million Jews in Europe, known as the Holocaust or the Shoah, was the crime that was harder than any other to minimize or set off against. For this reason and because of the ways in which this crime was conceived, organized, and committed, its very existence – or its magnitude or purpose – was questioned by extreme pro-Nazi and/or anti-Semitic circles, so that, in this case, we are not talking about mere revisionism but about negationism (Holocaust denial).

Holocaust deniers use arsenal of revisionism for creating relativist confusion, concealing facts and associations that do not fit the predetermined conclusion and overstating others. In addition, they also go a step further by denying historical facts, falsifying evidence, misinterpreting sources, and generally disregarding any scientifically rigorous historical methodology. The constant refrain is that the Holocaust is a Zionist conspiracy to target Germany and hide the crimes of the Allies in the Second World War. Since the 1960s, when the Holocaust denier industry began, with works referencing each other, the evidence for the organization and execution of the Holocaust has proliferated (from testimonies of victims and perpetrators to Nazi archives that existed in the Soviet Union and more). Nevertheless, Holocaust deniers insist on the same claims, proving in this way that it is a predetermined verdict, a programmatic characteristic and tendency for modern neo-Nazism.

The methods followed by the denialists, and revisionists in general, were able to develop and gain access to academia in an environment and situated within the timeframe of the rise of relativism and even agnosticism, which became more commonly known as postmodernism. According to the historian Richard Evans, in the postmodern intellectual climate that prevailed mainly in the United States from the mid-1970s onward (and which have been spread as is now evident in most of the Western world), more and more scholars were questioning whether texts possessed any fixed meaning, arguing instead that they were made meaningful by the reader, and attacks on the Western rationalist tradition had become commonplace. In this atmosphere, the activities of Holocaust deniers were also expanded and intensified, since absolute relativism left no criteria for refuting these fascist and racist views, and criticism against them was perceived as an "attack on freedom of speech" (Evans, 2009).

The best known case to readers is probably that of (pseudo)historian David Irving, who sued historian Deborah Lipstadt in 1996 when she criticized him for falsifying sources about the Holocaust. As a result, the trial turned into a scholarly examination of his writings. Lipstadt's accusations were proven, and he was described in the court judgment as an active Holocaust denier, anti-Semite, and racist, associated with far-right extremists promoting neo-Nazism. Historian Richard Evans, a key witness at the trial said: "if by historian we mean someone who investigates to discover the truth about the past and give us as accurate a representation of it as possible, then Irving is not a historian." Irving himself, a few years later, was arrested and sentenced in Austria to 3 years in prison for Holocaust denial. The trials and convictions of Irving and others have opened up the issue of litigation as a way of dealing with Holocaust deniers and other revisionists, turning the judiciary into the arbiter of history. While not all cases are the same and given the difference between revisionism and "denialism" seen above, it is true that such trials offer publicity to individuals who would otherwise be rather marginal and inaccessible to the wider public (Fleischer, 2008).

A similar case of publicity was recently witnessed in Greece, with the case of the prosecution of the historian Heinz Richter under the anti-racist law, for his findings on the Battle of Crete. He alleged "chivalrous attitude" of the German paratroopers and "barbarity" on the part the Cretan Resistance fighters. The charge was dropped, predictably, but the publicity it gave Richter encouraged him to new revisionist adventures by questioning the German occupation debt to Greece, with a dash of anti-Semitism about Greek Jews who received priority reparations. He even achieved a new level of racist discourse by characterizing Cretans as a "different race."

Let us now return to the Holocaust. There seem to be no real barriers between the outright deniers and the revisionists. The prominent spokesman for the latter, Ernst Nolte, while not denying the commission of the Holocaust, had repeatedly acknowledged the "honorable intentions" of the deniers, and that their arguments had merit and should be heeded. Lipstadt, in an interview, made a pertinent observation: "Historians like the German Ernst Nolte are in some ways more dangerous than the deniers. Nolte is a first-rate anti-Semite who tries to rehabilitate Hitler by saying he was no worse than Stalin. But he is careful not to be explicit on denying the Holocaust. Holocaust deniers make Nolte's life easier. With their radical arguments they have pulled the center (centrist arguments) a little more to their side. Consequently, a less radical extremist like Nolte is closer to the center, which makes him more dangerous" (interview archived in https://shorturl.at/1upmu, see Deborah Lipstadt on Wikipedia).

BACK TO THE ROOTS

In Germany, revisionist efforts were primarily aimed at mitigating the pan-European ramifications of Nazism, attributing their suffering to external sources, particularly the socialist revolution in Russia. Conversely, in France, the focus of revisionism was to address and diminish the impact of their own revolutionary history. Owing to the significant historical gravitas of the French Revolution, the revision of 20th-century history, alongside the demonization of communism, was orchestrated by tracing the lineage of revolutions from Russia back to France. This historical journey positioned the French Revolution as the "womb of totalitarianism," suggesting that the origins of totalitarian regimes could be discerned within the revolutionary fervor that characterized this pivotal moment in French history. This perspective not only reevaluates the legacy of the French Revolution but also influences the interpretation of subsequent revolutionary movements, particularly in their relation to the emergence of the so-called totalitarian states.

Consequently, in France, the revision of the history of the revolutions essentially led to the demarcation of liberalism from the historical legacy of the revolutions. Typically, while in Germany, revisionism was mainly associated with the new right, in France, on the contrary, it was represented by former communists and leftists who renounced their political past and aligned themselves with (neo-)liberal orthodoxy. This political inversion led to a revision of the schema of historical progress, which had to carefully eliminate the revolutionary processes as the catalyst of history moving forward from one social order to another. This intellectual maneuver culminated in the portrayal of political and economic liberalism as the optimal and, ostensibly, the sole viable world order. Such a depiction inherently positions both communism and fascism as historical aberrations from the normative claims of liberalism.

Historian François Furet, a former member of the French Communist Party and an expert on the history of the French Revolution, was the emblematic figure of this course. While Furet continued a narrative that maintained history with an orientation toward progress, however, only in which neither revolutions nor, of course, a different social system no longer has a place. Beginning with a critique of the most radical phase of the French Revolution, he led to a wholesale rejection of its necessity for the advent of modern democracy and to a denunciation of it as a "derailment" from a normal path to liberalism. Traverso observes that Furet maintains a liberal narrative as teleological as the Marxist one, yet the Revolution lost "the glamour of the epic milestone in the march of Progress" in order to be presented as a "pathological condition" (Traverso, 2016, p. 82).

The inquiry into the foundational causes behind the emergence of revolutions occupies a critical space in the discourse of historical and sociopolitical studies. What is really the reason for the existence of revolutions? Once economic, social, and even political reasons are rejected, the outbreak of revolutions can be reduced to "ideological" reasons, the obsessions of a minority with increasingly obscure aims and practices. For Furet, revolution, whether French or Russian, is due to ideology, and the regimes it wants to install are "ideocratic." The Terror of the French Revolution is attributed to these ideological reasons and is presented as the model for all subsequent bloody revolutions, and especially as the model for Bolshevik violence.

Since Furet had initiated the idea of equating the two emblematic revolutions (ignoring all differences and especially the material conditions in each case), this paved the way for a series of generalizations and identifications to create a passe-partout model of revolution. For Furet's disciple Patrice Gueniffey, revolutions are characterized by "endless terrorism" and "serial killing of victims" based on a scenario that "has not ceased to repeat itself for two centuries" (Traverso, 2016, p. 85). The war in the Vendée could be presented as a precursor to the communist "genocides" and the violence of the French Revolution more generally as an inspiration for the Bolshevik massacres.

Once the material conditions were removed, history became a ballast (and trial) of intentions, a collection of voluntarist acts. The concept of ideology, which was an argument of a conservative historiography, was to be a great success in liberal historiography against the concept and fact of revolution. The causes of revolutions could be categories such as ideology, psychosis, passion, fanaticism, violence, and terrorism. The next, and last, stage was the presentation of communism simply as a criminal idea and practice. From The Past of an Illusion (Furet, 1995) where fascism and communism were merely "brief episodes, framed by that which they wished to destroy": liberal democracy to the Black Book of Communism (1997) – edited, after Furet's death, by Stéphane Courtois (a former leftist) – where communism is presented as a criminal phenomenon, the cause of millions of deaths, no longer because of the dynamics of revolutions but as a planned crime. With Courtois, however, one can see a further drift toward a radical view, completely detached from reality and into a constellation of pathology, viewing communism as the biggest crime of imaginable. All the victims of wars and revolutions are added up to attribute them to the criminal nature of communism, thus proving that the latter is worse than fascism.

ELEMENTS OF A DECLARED REVISIONIST PROJECT

The Greek version of the revisionist current has been identified mainly with the work of political scientists Stathis Kalyvas and Nikos Marantzidis. Besides, they themselves claim this status as particularly honorable, as the essence of the scientific approach (Καλύβας & Μαραντζίδης, 2015). However, as in the other cases we have already presented, their revision consists not so much in formulating new questions and re-evaluating interpretative schemes, which do indeed constitute the essence of the research. Rather, their attempts focus in enshrining preconceived schemes with a specific, objectively political, purpose: the condemnation of the left as a priori totalitarian, if not criminal, force. After all, in the introduction to their latest synthetic work on the Greek Civil War, they clearly proclaim the goal of deconstructing the dominant myths, which happen to be "almost exclusively of leftist persuasion." We will not proceed to an exhaustive critique of a specific work nor of their now long-lasting course, but in the context of our historiographical tour, we will make a final stop to see how all the above historiographical developments have influenced the Greek version of revisionism.

From the outset, Kalyvas-Marantzidis' research aimed on the documentation of leftist, "red" violence during the occupation period, as a prelude to the presentation of the entire 1940s as a bloody attempt by the Kommounistiko Komma Ellados (KKE), that is Communist Party of Greece (CPG) to seize power. Adopting the technique of body counting – in selected areas and with selected sources – Kalyvas tried to document the greater lethality of leftist violence in Argolida and Messinia, ignoring the historical context, which was none other than the harsh Nazi occupation. It thus applied, in the Greek case, the scapegoating of the Black Book of Communism, established by Courtois, under whom Nikos Marantzidis studied, the other member of the group.

It is noteworthy to mention that an alternative periodization of the Civil War is presented, the beginning of which, for Kalyvas-Marantzidis, must be placed in 1943 during the Occupation. This is done in order to attribute the initial responsibility for the Civil War to the aforementioned leftist violence. Its onset in 1946 – as is generally accepted by the historical community – is less satisfactory as responsibility can be attributed to the white terrorism of the post-Varkizian (the Varkiza Treaty which the resistance forces were agreed to be disarmed) period or even earlier. For the same reason, Nolte posited the inception of the "European Civil War" not in 1914, a year traditionally associated with the unleashing of European barbarism previously reserved for other regions of the world, but rather in 1917 with the Russian Revolution. He argued that this event marked a pivotal shift, legitimizing Nazism as a reactionary response to the upheavals initiated by the Russian Revolution. This perspective highlights a reinterpretation of 20th-century European history, emphasizing the Russian Revolution's critical role in precipitating ideological extremities, thus providing justification for Nazism.

By contrast, if for Nolte Nazism and the war of extermination in the East was a logical response to the Bolshevik threat, then why not render the so-called Security Battalions (armed bodies formed by the Nazis during the Greek occupation), as Kalyvas–Marantzides suggest, an understandable reaction to the violence of the left? In this particular case, Kalyvas–Marantzidis cite a series of causes, social, economic, political (we will not find corresponding analyses for the action of the left – there, as we have seen above, ideology is sufficient) for the formation of the Security Battalions, which ultimately contribute to anti-communism, as a logical reaction to the communist threat.

There is also a great similarity between the declarations of Kalyvas–Marantzidis and those of the German New Right. From the era of the Dialogue on History through newspapers in 2004 to the Civil Passion, the duo boasts of bringing the new to historical research, boldly and confidently, against the hierarchies and the regimented logic expressed by history professors such as George Margaritis, Hagen Fleischer or Elias Nikolakopoulos. They characterize historical interpretations that do not fit their purposes (and which had indeed overturned decades of regime narratives) as politically targeted concepts without historical documentation, in short, as "the mythology of the left." They did not fail, like their German counterparts, to denounce their silencing at every opportunity and to present themselves as victims while their promotion in the mainstream media and other well-established institutions is systematic.

Ultimately, what is expressed throughout Europe with the advent of historical revisionist attempts is also valid for Greece: objectively, the political goal is the denigration and demonization of the left and resistance forces in the past and its marginalization in the political present. Not so much of the specific left parties of today but as a symbol in general of the value of social resistance, of revolution as a progressive process, of the vision and possibility of a more just social organization. Communism for Furet is an illusion; for Marantzides, it is a utopia that has lost its rationality (Marantzidis, 2010).

Theories about the end of history have finally passed away in the growing global crisis and the emergence of new geopolitical battlegrounds, but history itself is not passing away, no matter how much it may be exorcised. "Wars of Memory" and "History as a Battlefield" are typical titles of books that attempt to describe the struggle to interpret the past with the prize being political domination of the present. The revision of history is in full swing, at the state level, in academia, in public history, in the formation of collective memory. Assurances of scientific objectivity and impartiality cannot hide the high political stakes. The science of history, through conflicts, continues its long journey to understand the human past with ever more evidence, deeper interpretations, broader schemes. Beyond revisionism and negativism, new substantive interpretive schemes are being put together to shed more light on the past, that is, on the future.

REFERENCES

El País. (2023). Orbán blasts the European Union on the anniversary of Hungary's 1956 anti-Soviet uprising. [online]. https://english.elpais.com/international/2023-10-23/orban-blasts-the-european-union-on-the-anniversary-of-hungarys-1956-anti-soviet-uprising.html. Accessed on March, 2023.

Evans, R. J. (2009). *Για την υπεράσπιση της ιστορίας*. Σαββάλας.

Fleischer, H. (2008). *Πόλεμοι μνήμης: Ο Δεύτερος Παγκόσμιος Πόλεμος στη σύγχρονη δημόσια ιστορία* [Memory wars: The second world war in contemporary public history]. Nefeli.

Furet, F. (1995). Europe after utopianism. *Journal of Democracy*, 6(1), 79–89.

Hobsbawm, E. (2003). *Η εποχή των άκρων. Ο Σύντομος Εικοστός Αιώνας 1914–1991*. Θεμέλιο.

Καλύβας, Σ. Ν., & Μαραντζίδης, Ν. (2015). *Εμφύλια Πάθη. 23 ερωτήσεις και απαντήσεις για τον Εμφύλιο*. Μεταίχμιο.

Κωστόπουλος, Τ. (2005). *Η αυτολογοκριμένη μνήμη: Τα Τάγματα Ασφαλείας και η μεταπολεμική εθνικοφροσύνη*. Φιλίστωρ.

Marantzidis, N. (2010). *I istoria tu DSE* [The history of DSE]. Alexandria Publishing.

Μαραντζίδης, Ν. (2010). *Δημοκρατικός Στρατός Ελλάδας*. Αλεξάνδρεια.

Nolte, E. (2000). *La guerre civile européenne 1917–1945. National-socialisme et bolchevisme*. Éditions des Syrtes.

President of Poland. (2023). President visits Hungary on Friday to celebrate bilateral friendship. https://www.president.pl/news/president-visits-hungary-on-friday-to-celebrate-bilateral-friendship,36674. Accessed on April, 2023.

Traverso, E. (2016). *Η Ιστορία ως πεδίο μάχης. Ερμηνεύοντας τις βιαιότητες του 20ού αιώνα*. εκδόσεις του Εικοστού Πρώτου.

Wolin, R. (2007). *Η γοητεία του ανορθολογισμού. Το ειδύλλιο της διανόησης με τον φασισμό. Από τον Νίτσε στον μεταμοντερνισμό*. Πόλις.

3

THE GREEK CIVIL WAR IN FILM

PANAGIOTIS DENDRAMIS

University of Patras, Greece

Keywords: Films; history in cinema; new Greek cinema; Angelopoulos; revisionism in films

INTRODUCTION

It was the year 1977 when French historian Marc Ferro published his iconic book "Cinéma et Histoire." Within its pages, he highlighted the numerous intersecting elements between cinema and history (Ferro, 1988). His work would constitute a landmark for the advancement of the academic field of Film Studies and in particular its interconnection with aspects of historical research. Ferro's study largely focused on the cinematic depiction of events and historical figures from early 20th century Russia and the USSR, such as *Battleship Potemkin* (1925) and *Chapaev* (1934). Yet, during the same decade – that of the 1970s – a more recent historical period of another country would start to be represented on the silver screen, causing thus intense discussions and in some cases even strong debates.

That period was the Greek Civil War, which took place mainly during the second-half of the 1940s, following the country's involvement in the Second World War on the first-half of the same decade. Its impact on Greece's subsequent politics, economy and foreign affairs, as well as on its society and morals, has made it a quintessential factor that shaped the country's modern identity. It has become a controversial subject that continues to provoke fierce political confrontations to this day, while at the same it attracts the vivid interest of historical research, especially during the recent years, domestically and abroad (Close, 2014; Margaritis, 2002). Within this context, some filmmakers would attempt to depict aspects and themes of the Creek Civil War in cinema, as a representational form of art and communication that uses audiovisual means for the narration of stories, many of which are based on real events. Yet this process would prove difficult and complexed, affected to a large extent by the special historical and sociopolitical circumstances or the ideological conceptions created by Civil War itself.

CONCURRENT DEPICTIONS

Cinema was introduced to Greek audience for the first time on November 28, 1896, exactly 11 months after its initial presentation by the Lumière Brothers at the "Salon Indien du Grand Café" in Paris (Delveroudi, 1999, p. 389). The first feature film, an adaptation of the famous pastoral play "Golfo" written by Spyridon Peresiadis, was made in 1915. Yet during the 1930s, film production in Greece had come to a standstill, due to the effects from the Great Depression at the country's economy, the political instability, as well the incapability of native filmmakers to adapt to the technological changes of the medium itself, such as the introduction of sound (Karalis, 2012, pp. 31–33). In 1939, Filopimin Finos shot his first film *To tragoudi tou horismou* (The Parting Song, 1939) which was also the first fully sound feature film made in Greece. Four years later, in the midst of the country's Nazi Occupation, he produced his next film, *I Foni tis Kardias* (The Voice of the Heart, 1943), through his then newly formed production unit, "Finos Film." Finos and his company would become pivotal figures for the development of Greek cinema during the following years and would dominate the domestic film market until the mid-1970s. The boost toward the rebirth of Greek cinema that Finos initiated then coincided with the dramatic historical events of the time, and was inevitably affected by them.

Finos, who had previously served in the Albanian front during the Greco-Italian War of 1940–1941 as a photographer-cinematographer for the Greek Army (Zervas, 2003, p. 73), was arrested by the Nazis in 1944, along with his father, on the accusation of providing help to the Greek resistance guerrillas. They were both sentenced to death, yet the Nazis executed only his father. This traumatic experience deeply affected Finos for the rest of his life (Finosfilm.com, n.d.). On October of the same year, German troops withdrew from Athens and gradually from the rest of Greece. Finos decided to document the liberation of Athens with his camera. He succeeded to capture several important events, such as the downhaul of the Swastika flag from the Acropolis, the celebrating crowd in the city's central streets, the ELAS partisans in Kesariani neighborhood, the aftermath of the atrocities conducted by the conquerors and their collaborators, the arrival of the first British troops and that of the Greek battleship "Averoff" (Vidakis, 2021). Finos and his colleagues in "Finos Film" edited the footage into one film and made a voice-over, with the intention of showing it as a newsreel in Athenian cinema halls, celebrating thus the end of the war and occupation in a spirit of reconciliation. Nevertheless, the quick deterioration of the political atmosphere that led to *Dekemvriana* (December Events) put a halt to their project. This film would remain unseen by the public until 1999, when director and researcher Roviros Manthoulis discovered a copy of it in an American film archive and showed it as part of a TV documentary about the Civil War (Mendrinos, 2021).

Finos's perception about politics and his call for reconciliation between the two opposing parties would become more evident a few years later, when the civil war was already on full scale. He decided to produce Οι Γερμανοί ξανάρχονται (The Nazis strike again, 1948), based on a play of the same name that had been staged 2 years before in "Rex" theatre of Athens (Stamatopoulou, 2017, p. 135). The play as well as its adaptation were written by Alekos Sakellarios and Hristos Giannakopoulos, with the former being also the director of the film. Many of the main characters were also played by the same actors as those on stage, like the protagonist Vasilis Logothetidis and his wife in the movie, Nitsa Tsaganea. The subtitle of the film called it a "satirical nightmare" and it is indeed a dark comedy that takes place in an Athenian neighborhood, a few time after the end of the Nazi occupation, a period that coincides with the one that preceded the conflict of Dekemvriana. In the midst of the political tensions between Left- and Right-wing supporters, a peaceful Athenian, Theodoros, has a dream in which Adolph Hitler, after having managed to survive World War 2, decides to lead again his Nazi troops against Greece. This unexpected development forces Greeks to reunite, as during the war, in order to defend themselves. As with the play, the film was a big financial success for Finos Film. At the same time it expressed the feelings of that part of the population coming especially from petit bourgeois or middle class backgrounds, that remained neutral toward the conflict. Those people, tired from the ongoing hardship and instability since the beginning of the war (as well as before that in many cases), wished above all for a closure of the past predicament, in order to pursue their fortune in the postwar era. Contrary, the film received severe criticism from the press who supported one side or the other, such as *Rizospastis*, the official newspaper of the Communist Party of Greece (KKE), and *Estia*, a newspaper that was aligned with conservative and even nationalistic cycles (Mouratidis, 2009, pp. 30–47).

This Finos production would become the only fiction film that openly commented on the turmoil caused by the civil strife during the time it occurred. Many years passed until another attempt to represent this era would appear on screen. Nonetheless, the clash was cinematically covered by both sides. Footage from various aspects of the ongoing confrontation in Northern Greece was documented between 1946 and 1949, in order to produce newsreels and propaganda films. Foreign film companies like the "British Pathé" and correspondents connected to American journals and state agencies created such films. These newsreels were shown in cinema venues before or after the projection of feature films, in support of the official Greek government and its allies, Great Britain at first and then later on, the USA (British Pathé, 2014). Additionally, films in favor of the Hellenic Army were also produced in Greece. Film archives from the period that have been preserved include scenes from the war front, inspection of troops by officers, tours in the Pindos area by politicians and King Paul or visits by members of the royal family – especially Queen Frederica – at the Child Cities (Paidoupoleis), the network of camps for children that were constructed under her supervision (Hellenic National AudioVisual Archive, 1947–1949). The voice-over that accompanies some of them offers an indicative example of the propaganda speech that was used on behalf of the formal regime and its supporters.

On the other side, the pro-communist Democratic Army of Greece (DSE) had formed its own small cinematographic unit. Its members were the later prominent theatre director Yiorgos Sevastikoglou, Apostolos Mousouris, Fotis Matsakas, and Manos Zaharias (dse.kke.gr, n.d.). The latter, a student at the French National Film School IDHEC at the time, managed to illegally arrive at the territory controlled by DSE forces, bringing along with him from Paris two cameras and film stock. Despite the difficult conditions they had to overcome, by combining military practice and filming at the same time, they managed to document many aspects of the Democratic Army's activities, as well as those of the Provisional Democratic Government, the administration declared by the Communist Party of Greece. A part of this footage was used for the production of the documentary: *Η αλήθεια για τα παιδιά της Ελλάδας* (The Truth About the Children of Greece, 1948). This film was created as a response to the accusations by DSE opponents for the practice of "paidomazoma," i.e., the removal of children from the region under its control. As with Queen Frederica's Camps, the Provisional Democratic Government decided in many cases to take children from the Pindos villages and resettle them in special camps in

Eastern Bloc countries. It is estimated that around 30,000 children were removed by the Democratic Army (Bærentzen, 1987, pp. 147–155). In order to justify this controversial action, the film emphasizes on the hardships and the dangers by the continuous warfare in which the children and their families were exposed to. According to its narrative, the responsible for this situation was the Greek Government and its western allies, who succeeded Nazi occupation and Metaxas's dictatorship before that, in the suppression and injustice against the local population. The film includes scenes from the everyday life of the children in the camps, in which they are presented well nurtured and educated, safe, and happy under the care of the Communist Party's allies (TVXS.gr, 2011).

After the collapse of the DSE resistance in 1949 and the insurgents' withdrawal in Albania and Yugoslavia, the cinematic unit was deactivated. Sevastikoglou and Zaharias managed to arrive at the USSR, where they would pursue successful careers as directors in theatre and cinema, respectively. Their documentary, along with the rest of the footage that they had shot during their service in the ranks of the Democratic Army, would be considered lost for many years. A copy of the film was again found by Roviros Manthoulis in the 1990s, in a private collection in France. A few years later, KKE released through *Rizospastis*, a DVD of a slightly different version of the same film, that had been also found in its archives. Since then, some additional audiovisual footage has been discovered in the party's archives, has been restored and presented to the public. A part of it can be seen through the website that has been created for the presentation of the archival material concerning the history of DSE at: dse.kke.gr/. This finding comes as a reaffirmation of Zaharias's claim that a large portion of the footage that he shot along with his comrades is still missing and needs to be retrieved, so it could enrich historical research and our understanding of that particular period (Zaharias, 2011, p. 12).

1950–1975: TIME OF CONCEALMENT

The end of the 1940s coincided with that of the Civil War. Within the context of the Cold War that ensued over the following few decades, Greece became a member of NATO in 1952 and would be considered as a stronghold of the West (Europe and the USA) on its borderline with the communist states of the Balkan peninsula. All these had a decisive effect in the country's domestic politics. The end of the fight was marked by the victory of the right wing and its absolute dominance in Greece's political affairs. This was accompanied by the prosecution of its opponents for almost 25 years, from 1950 until 1974, when the military Junta that had seized power in 1967 collapsed. Even before the dictatorship though, the nature of the regime was lacking democratic elements. A large part of the population was suspected as being communist sympathizer and therefore was treated as internal enemy. Thousands of left-wing supporters were held in prison, sent into internal exile on deserted islands like Makronisos, and in some cases – such as Nikos Belloyanis and Grigoris Labrakis – even lost their lives (Richter, 2020). During the same period, Greek cinema experienced an unprecedented growth. With "Finos Film" as its leading company and many others following, film production – as well as film attendance in cinemas – reached its peak, with more than 100 movies per year from the mid-1960s until the beginning of the 1970s (Sotiropoulou, 1989, p. 82). The majority of them included comedies and melodramas. There were also some "foustanellas," the native genre that involved bucolic romances and mountainous adventures that gradually gave their place to the "Greek film musical," in the 1960s (Papadimitriou, 2005).

Another popular sub-genre of the era was that of the war drama, which was mainly inspired from the Second World War. These films focused on stories either from the Greco-Italian War or from the Nazi Occupation and the Resistance of the Greeks (Andritsos, 2005). What can be easily observed is that besides the period of the first-half of the 1940s, there was a blank in film production concerning the second-half. The years between 1950 and 1975, widely known as the "golden era" of Greek cinema, were characterized by the strong reluctance of native filmmakers to approach not only the issue of Civil War but also politics in general. The main reason for that was the existence of a strict censorship, official and unofficial, that made them extremely cautious toward any attempt to depict related subjects. Only indirect or politically neutral references can be found in certain films, like *Η κόρη μου η σοσιαλίστρια* (My Daughter, the Socialist, 1966). This film, made also by Alekos Sakellarios, places the political climate of its time as the backdrop of yet another typical romance between Aliki Vougiouklaki and Dimitris Papamihail, Greek cinema's superstar couple of that period. On the contrary, when another renowned film star of the era, Alekos Alexandrakis, made his directorial debut with *Συνοικία «Το Όνειρο»* (Dream Neighborhood, 1961) he encountered serious obstacles. Inspired by Italian Neorealism, Alexandrakis decided to make a film about the grim reality that many Greeks were coping with on a daily basis. Even though the film did not have any direct reference to the Civil War, its commentary on social issues along with the fact that many members of its cast – as Alexandrakis himself – were known left-wing supporters, caused reactions of behalf of the regime. Initially, parastatals posed problems throughout the film's production. Then, during its premiere at Thessaloniki Film Festival, the director and his colleagues were bullied by an angry mob of right-wing extremists. Finally, in order to get the approval for circulating in the cinemas, it was censored to such an extent that Alexandrakis renounced it as his work (Zouboulakis, 2011).

1975-1990: CIVIL WAR AND NEW GREEK CINEMA

The Turkish invasion of Cyprus and the occupation of its northern part in 1974 led to a swift political turmoil in Greece that resulted at the overthrow of the military Junta and the restoration of democracy. The next year, director Theo Angelopoulos made his third feature film, Ο θίασος (The Travelling Players, 1975). This marked a turning point on how the Greek Civil War, and also history and politics in general, would be approached by Greek filmmakers afterward. The film revolves around a wandering group of actors from 1939 until 1952. Through their stories, Angelopoulos presents the country's major historical developments of that period. Events from the Civil War appeared in the film, as well as those that preceded and followed it. Angelopoulos openly commented on the causes of the conflict, highlighting for the first time the left-wing viewpoint on Greece's recent history. The conservative government of Konstantinos Karamanlis that had succeeded the dictatorship prevented the film from entering in the Cannes festival, even though it had already garnered international acclaim. The excuse for this decision was that it portrayed the historical events one sided, and if it won the Palme d'Or, this could provoke a new round of political tensions. Nevertheless, Ο θίασος managed to win numerous other awards and is today considered amongst the most important films of the latter half of the 20th century (Horton, 1999, pp. 102–126).

Angelopoulos was one of the prominent figures of a new wave of Greek directors that opposed the mainstream film production and followed the esthetic trends of similar cinematic movements of that era, like the French Nouvelle Vague, the New German Cinema, and the Czechoslovak New Wave. They were attributed with the name: *New Greek Cinema* or NEK (acronym of its Greek translation: Νέος Ελληνικός Κινηματογράφος). Besides their common stance toward filmmaking, the members of this group shared the same ideological beliefs. The majority of them supported the Left in its various versions, from revolutionary Marxism-Leninism to radical Social Democracy, as it was expressed during that time by PASOK

(Valoukos, 2011). In accordance with the highly politicized atmosphere of the mid-1970s, known also as "Metapoilitefsi," some of those filmmakers sought to shine a light on the country's recent past, filtered through their ideological perspective.

Pantelis Voulgaris, another major director of NEK, made *Happy Day* (1976), a film shot at Makronisos, one of the deserted islands that was used as concentration camps for political prisoners from 1947 until 1974. Coming from a leftist family, Voulgaris had been imprisoned himself there a few months before, during the last period of the military Junta, and was released when the dictatorship ended. He decided to return to this infamous place, in order to make a film adaptation of the novel "O limos *(The Famine)*" by Andreas Fragias, another ex-political prisoner of Makronisos. As with the book, the film avoids making any specific references to place, time, or political context. In that way, its message transcends spatio-temporal boundaries and casts a critical gaze upon the irrationality of imprisonment and totalitarianism in general (Kranakis, 2015). However, its connection with situations that were established during the Civil War and continued to exist after it was more than obvious for the Greek audience.

The next year, Angelopoulos would create another film with references to the fratricide strife. Οι κυνηγοί (The Hunters, 1977) depicts a group of bourgeois hunters that stumbles upon a body of a dead partisan that has been preserved by the snow. They decide to take him back with them to their resort, so the police can make an inquiry about his case. What follows is a symbolic account of the precedent years, from the interstate conflict till the military coup d'état of 1967. With this film, Angelopoulos completed his "historical trilogy," which had started with Οι μέρες του '36 (Days of '36, 1972). In those three films, he attempted a critical presentation of Greece's political history of the previous four decades. Angelopoulos would return to the issue of the Civil War during the next decade, in a more indirect manner. At his next cinematic triptych, the "trilogy of silence" [Ταξίδι στα Κύθηρα (Voyage to Cythera, 1984), Ο μελισσοκόμος (The Beekeeper, 1986), and Τοπίο στην ομίχλη (Landscape in the Mist, 1988)], he replaced his interest about Big History with the personal stories of people affected by it. His characters try to overcome the outside difficulties and their inner psychological traumas, caused by the long lasted political dispute of the past (Horton, 1999, pp. 127–160). A similar approach was also applied by Voulgaris in his Τα πέτρινα χρόνια (Stone Years, 1985). Based on a true story from his family, it follows a communist couple and the hardships that they start to face in the aftermath of the Civil War. They spend the next two decades mostly apart, both incarcerated as political prisoners. Yet the director, known moreover for his humanistic vision, focuses mainly on the relationship between the two and the emotional burden they have to overcome from the harsh conditions that they are exposed to, in order to be together again.

Besides these two acclaimed filmmakers of NEK, other directors who were also associated with the group created movies with direct or indirect references to the Civil War, during the 1980s. In the beginning of the decade, Nikos Tzimas made Ο άνθρωπος με το γαρύφαλλο (The Man with the Carnation, 1980). His film presents the story of Nikos Beloyiannis, a leading cadre of the Greek Communist Party who in 1952 was accused of treason and was sentenced to death. His trial and execution caused a wide international concern about the political liberties in Greece, with many intellectuals making appeals for clemency. In order to honor Beloyannis, Pablo Picasso created a sketch named "The Man with the Carnation," based on a photo of him during his trial. Even though the main events of the movie take place sometime after the end of the clash, they nonetheless appear as its consequences. For this reason, Tzimas chooses to include also scenes from the political conflict of the period 1946–1949. His film uses simple narrative codes that the audience was accustomed to from mainstream film production. Yet in this case, they serve a different purpose. Its premise along with the timing of its release – shortly before the elections of 1981, when the right wing lost from PASOK for the first time – made the film a huge commercial success and one of the highest grossing productions of that year (Soldatos, 1999, p. 222). It should be noted here that as with Tzimas's film, all the previously mentioned works of Angelopoulos and Voulgaris were also the highest grossing Greek movies during the year of their release (Andritsos, 2016, pp. 4–8). This is an indication that besides their artistic value, they were also responding to the audience's need for a cinematic depiction of the late political history of the country.

The same year as Tzimas, Pavlos Tassios made Παραγγελιά (Parangelia!, 1980), a film about the real story of Nikos Koemtzis, an ex-convict who attacked a company of police officers in a tavern, when they provoked him by dancing with the song he had "ordered." His attack resulted in the killing of three people and the injury of another seven. In the film, Tassios makes a number of remarks about Koemtzis's childhood, when both his parents were persecuted for being left-wing supporters, and how this affected his personality. Similar references to the Civil War can be seen in Μάθε παιδί μου γράμματα (Learn How to Read and Write, Son, 1981), a comedy written and directed by Thodoros Maragos. In his movie, the quite life of a conservative village in the Peloponnese is disrupted by the unveiling of a monument for the victims of the Occupation, when it is noted that the name of a communist partisan who was also killed has been omitted (Galanou, 2011).

Nevertheless, this preoccupation of some filmmakers – in particular members of NEK – with the Civil War started to be received more skeptically as the decade of the 1980s was evolving. For example, it was satirized by Nikos Perakis the following year, in his film Άρπα Κόλλα (Arpa Colla, 1982). Andritsos points out that 1982 can be considered as a turning point on the representation of the Civil War (Andritsos, 2016, p. 9). After PASOK came to power, numerous reforms took place in many aspects of the political and social spectrum. Among them, the official recognition of the Resistance in August 23, 1982 was an act that was interpreted as atonement for left-wing partisans and the hardships they were put into after the end of the war. Greek society seemed to transform and gradually entering an era of political stability and economic comfort, as a member of the EU. Within this environment, new approaches on the issue of the civil conflict were introduced. In 1984, Η κάθοδος των εννιά (The Descent of the Nine, 1984) was made by Christos Siopahas. Based on a novel by Thanasis Valtinos, the film follows the group of the last DSE fighters on the Peloponnese, as they try to make their way to the sea, in order to escape their enemies. Beneath the struggle for survival, the rebels also have to overcome their disappointment from the outcome of the rebellion, something that causes doubts about the decisions of the party's leadership and consequently tensions amongst them. The same year, Nikos Tzimas returned with Τα χρόνια της θύελλας (Against the Storm, 1984). In this film, Tzimas examines the whole decade of the 1940s, through the story of two friends. It starts from the war in the Albanian front, after the collapse of which the two men, who have fought there together, decide to join ELAS, the military branch of the left-wing National Liberation Front (EAM). During the Civil War they become fighters of the DSE and after the defeat, try to escape captivity and death.

At the second-half of the 1980s four more movies came out with stories from the Civil War era. Yet none of them portrayed the actual fighting between the two sides in the mountains of Northern Greece. Instead, their creators chose to preoccupy themselves with less known side effects of the conflict. In Καραβάν Σαράι (Caravan Sarai, 1986) Tassos Psaras presents the story of a family from a village within the warzone, that due to the situation is forced to leave its home. They are sent to Thessaloniki and find shelter in an old building, a Caravan Serai as they were called, with hundreds of other refugees. It is there that the peaceful and neutral toward the conflict father of the family, along with his two children, has to overcome the difficulties of poverty, marginalization, and strict oppression on behalf of state officials (Psaras, 2018). Another film, also based on a book, was Τα παιδιά της Χελιδώνας (The Children of Helidona, 1987). Director Costas Vrettakos adapted the eponymous novel of Dionisis Haritopoulos, in which a journalist and a TV producer try to unravel the secrets of a family from Mountain Helidona. In order to do that they interview its members and visit their village. Each of the siblings presents his own version about the family's past and their traumatic experiences during the Civil War. On the other hand, the real events surrounding one of the first airplane hijackings in history are represented in O kloios (The Noose, 1987) by Kostas Koutsomytis. In 1948, six students, members of the Communist Party, decide to escape from Greece through a risky plan. They aboard a commercial flight from Athens to Thessaloniki and then ask the pilots to take them to Yugoslavia. The city of Thessaloniki is again the place of action in Φάκελος Πολκ στον αέρα (The Polk File, 1988). This docudrama from Dionysis Grigoratos deals with the unresolved murder case of George Polk, the American journalist who was found dead in the city's port, in the eve of his interview with DSE leader Markos Vafiadis. It should be noted here that the same story had already been presented twice in film, 10 and 20 years before, respectively: In Angelos Malliaris's Υπόθεση Πολκ (The Polk Case, 1978) and in Dimos Theos's Κιέριον (Kierion, 1968). Interestingly, the latter is today considered as the first feature film created by members of NEK (Valoukos, 2011, p. 108).

In contrast to the general trend of portraying the events of the fratricide clash from the perspective of the Left, *Eleni* (1985) was the only movie of the decade that spoke in favor of the opposite side. This was not the first film to do so. During the dictatorship, Δώστε τα χέρια (Shake Hands and Make Up, 1971) and Γράμμος (Grammos, 1971) had already provided examples of the conflict's representation in accordance with the far-right beliefs of the military regime. Yet these films had been treated, almost immediately after their release, as banal cinematic attempts to propagandize Junta (Voglis, 2006, pp. 108–111). *Eleni* on the other hand was an international production, financed mainly from American studios, with acclaimed British Peter Yates as the director and John Malkovich as the protagonist. It was based on the memoir of Greek – American journalist Nicolas Cage (or Nikos Gatzoyiannis in Greek), who during the fight, was forced to abandon his village in Pindos and whose mother had been killed by DSE. Its bleak portrayal of the insurgents and their leadership caused tensions from the production phase until its screening. The union of Greek cinematographers, who was strongly pro-Left, opposed to the shooting of the film in Greece, which was then done in Spain. Subsequently, when it premiered in the country's cinemas, KKE supporters organized demonstrations against it that in some cases resulted in violent disputes (mixanitouxronou.gr, n.d.).

1990–2020: REVISIONS AND REAPPROACHES

The decade of the 1980s ended with PASOK losing the elections of 1989, after 8 years of continuous governance. The coalition that was formed for a short term – until finally the right-wing New Democracy was unilaterally elected as government in 1990 – in order to manage the domestic political situation and the "Koskotas scandal," consisted of the political descendants of the Civil War's opponents. The joint government between Left and Right, along with the collapse of the socialist regimes in Eastern Europe, created new political conditions both internationally and within Greece. The next two decades the country would experience a further economic growth and political stability, characterized by the bipolar rotation in power between PASOK and New Democracy. In June of 2000 Greece joined the Eurozone and changed its currency from drachmas to euros, and in 2004 it held the Olympic Games in Athens. In this sociopolitical and economic framework, Greek cinema also tried to adapt itself by embracing new themes and more contemporary esthetic trends. For the filmmakers, the Greek Civil War appeared to be an obsolete subject (Flitouris, 2008, p. 404).

In 1995, Alexis Damianos, another notable figure of NEK, concluded his third feature film, *Ηνίοχος* (The Charioteer, 1995), on which he had been working on from the previous decade. The plot revolves around a teenage left-wing insurgent. We follow his daring life against the backdrop of the country's history from the 1940s to the 1990s. Damianos provides a new look on the particular historical era, that distinguishes him from the works of the past 20 years. Even though the narrative is clearly made from a leftist point of view, the movie seems to takes a somewhat critical stance on both sides. A similar attitude can be noticed in *Βασιλική* (Vasiliki, 1997) by Vagelis Serdaris, when a guerrilla fighter's wife and a police officer fall in love. Given the political circumstances, their affair is met with animosity by practically everyone, and they are eventually compelled to flee their community. The limited list of films dealing with the Civil War during this period also includes Ούλοι εμείς εφέντη (All of us master, 1998). Its director, Leonidas Vardaros, reveals a widely unknown, peripheral story from the conflict, that of a group of DSE fighters who continued the warfare for six more years, as they were isolated on the island of Ikaria. Finally, Tasos Psarras, in his *Η σκόνη που πέφτει* (Dust, 2004), focuses once again on the consequences of the confrontation that continue to affect people's lives in the present.

In contrast to the above, the end of the 00s and the beginning of the next decade marked the start of a severe recession for Greek economy and society. In December 2008, the assassination of 15-year-old student Alexis

Grigoropoulos by a policeman resulted in demonstrations and riots in the country's main cities. Through these protests, citizens and youth, in particular, expressed their distrust for the political system that had been established since 1974. This negative climate would escalate a couple of years later, when the Greek government, fearing bankruptcy, asked for the financial aid of the IMF, the European Central Bank and the European Commission, known as Troika. In exchange for their help, Greece accepted to reform its economy as well as many aspects of its state structure. Consequently, the country's GDP fell precipitously in the following years, affecting people's livelihoods in a variety of ways. This caused new social tensions and a revival of the political rivalry.

Within this context, two more movies about the Civil War came out. The first was Pantelis Voulgaris's Ψυχή Βαθιά (A Soul So Deep, 2009). In his 10th feature film, the experienced director opted to return to the theme of the national split, this time depicting the battlefield of Grammos Mountain during the final months of the struggle. The end of the hostilities is witnessed by two brothers who find themselves serving in the opposing armies. Two years later, Kostas Charalambous shot Δεμένη Κόκκινη Κλωστή (Tied Red Thread, 2011). In his film, the action takes place in a mountainous village, a few months before the official declaration of the civil conflict. Far right paramilitary gangs intimidate and murder left-wing supporters. At some point, one of them decides to retaliate, thus initiating a vicious cycle of violence. In his comparison of the two films, Kornetis points out that besides their different scale of production – the former being a large project and the latter an independent, low budget one – they also represent contrary perceptions on the matter. Voulgaris promotes the narrative of national reconciliation, while Charalambous seems to question it. Kornetis concludes that "while cinema was initially used as a means of fostering reconciliation, this changed dramatically following the onset of the crisis to the adoption of the trope of ultra-violence in depicting the conflict as both savage, but also somehow unresolved" (Kornetis, 2014, p. 111).

Next to these fiction films, a growing number of documentaries started to appear. This was a genre with which only few filmmakers had attempted to approach the Civil War in the past. One characteristic example came from Fotos Lambrinos, with Άρης Βελουχιώτης: Το δίλημμα (Aris Velouhiotis: The dilemma, 1981), a documentary that focuses on the life and personality of the captain of ELAS. Yet the last decades, changes in technology have facilitated the use of a digital, easy to handle and light enough to carry, audiovisual equipment. At the same time, the Greek audience has become more interested in the genre, thanks to the works of acclaimed documentarists like Eva Stefani and Fillipos Koutsaftis, in combination with its promotion from the festival circuit.

This has encouraged filmmakers to make documentaries in which they thoroughly examined certain aspects of the civil conflict. Amongst them, *Μακρόνησος* (Makronisos, 2008) by Ilias Giannakakis and Evi Karabatsou, *Άλλος δρόμος δεν υπήρχε* (There Was No Other Way, 2009) by Stavros Psyllakis, and *Τα Παιδιά του Εμφυλίου* (Fils De Grèce, 2015) from Dionysis Grigoratos, are some memorable mentions. A remarkable result also came from Alinda Dimitriou's trilogy about women's political activism from the 1940s to the fall of Junta: *Πουλιά στο Βάλτο* (Birds in the Mire, 2008), *Η ζωή στους βράχους* (Among the Rocks, 2009), and *Τα κορίτσια της βροχής* (The Girls of the Rain, 2012). The first two parts of the trilogy concern the years of the Resistance, the Civil War and its aftermath. Through the collective narration of events by female ex-militants of the DSE, the documentary offers a unique sample of oral history, given from a feminine perspective. Moreover, Dimitriou decided to put her work almost directly on "You Tube," in order to be open to the public for viewing. She was one of the first Greek filmmakers to do so (Dem edu, n.d.).

CONCLUSION

History and cinema are in constant interaction. Movies are made out of human stories and in return, they transform our image of the past. The Greek Civil War could be no exception to this tradition. As one of the most decisive historical events that affected the identity of modern Greece in multiple ways, it has been represented into films, through different modes and for various goals. In my text, I have offered a basic outline of this cinematic display. I moreover attempted to show the factors that played an important role for the production of these films, along with their impact and the reactions that they caused within Greek society. I have also examined the motives of their creators in connection to their social views and in conjunction with their creative vision. As it was pointed out, this dialectic relationship started at the time of the civil conflict, was later undermined for two decades due to political reasons, and then reappeared in the 1970s, having particular artistic and ideological characteristics. Since then it has continued to produce works from time to time that capture public attention.

REFERENCES

Andritsos, G. (2005). *Η Κατοχή και η Αντίσταση στον ελληνικό κινηματογράφο (1945–1966)*. Aigokeros.

Andritsos, G. (2016). Ο Εμφύλιος στις ελληνικές ταινίες μυθοπλασίας μεγάλου μήκους από το 1974 μέχρι το 1989. In *ανακοίνωση στο συνέδριο των Αρχείων Σύγχρονης Κοινωνικής Ιστορίας (ΑΣΚΙ): «Διαδρομές του Παρελθόντος. Ο εμφύλιος στη δημόσια ιστορία και μνήμη»*, 2 Δεκεμβρίου 2016, Αθήνα. https://www.academia.edu/42261483/. Accessed on July 27, 2022.

Bærentzen, L. (1987). The 'Paidomazoma' and the Queen's Camps. In L. Bærentzen, J. O. Iatrides, & O. Langwitz Smith (Eds.), *Studies in the history of the Greek civil war, 1945–1949* (pp. 127–158). Museum Tusculanum Press.

British Pathé. (2014). Fighting on northern frontier of Greece and British and Greek troops against communists (1947). [online videos]. https://www.britishpathe.com/video/fighting-on-northern-frontier-of-greece. https://www.britishpathe.com/video/british-and-greek-troops-against-communists. Accessed on July 27, 2022.

Close, D. H. (2014). *The origins of the Greek civil war*. Routledge.

Delveroudi, E. A. (1999). Κινηματογράφος: 1901–1922. In C. Hadziiossif (Ed.), *Ιστορία της Ελλάδας του 20ού αιώνα: Οι απαρχές 1900–1922* (pp. 388–399). Vivliorama.

Dem edu. (n.d.). Αλίντα Δημητρίου, Η ζωή στους βράχους. [online video]. https://www.youtube.com/watch?v=kTto2utNW_M&ab_channel=demedu. Accessed on July 27, 2022.

Dse.kke.gr. (n.d.). Αρχείο του κινηματογραφικού συνεργείου του ΔΣΕ. https://dse.kke.gr/. Accessed on July 27, 2022.

Eisenstein, S. (1925). *Battleship Potemkin*. [film]. Goskino.

Ferro, M. (1988). *Cinema and history*. Translated by Naomi Greene. Wayne State University Press.

Finos, F. (1939). *The Parting Song*. [film]. Finos Film.

Finosfilm.com. (n.d.). Φίνος: Ο «Πατριάρχης» του Ελληνικού Κινηματογράφου. http://finosfilm.com/finos. Accessed on July 27, 2022.

Flitouris, L. (2008). Ο εμφύλιος στο σελιλόιντ. Μνήμες νικητών και ηττημένων στον κινηματογράφο. In R. Van Boeschoten, T. Vervenioti, E. Voutira, K. V. Dalkavouris, & K. Bada (Eds.), *Μνήμες και λήθη του ελληνικού εμφυλίου πολέμου* (pp. 387–404). Epikentro.

Galanou, L. (2011, May 29). Μάθε Παιδί Μου Γράμματα. *Flix*. https://flix.gr/cinema/ma8e-paidi-moy-grammata.html. Accessed on July 27, 2022.

Hellenic National AudioVisual Archive. (1947–1949). Περιοδεία του Βασιλιά Παύλου στην περιοχή των πολεμικών επιχειρήσεων κατά τη διάρκεια του Εμφυλίου πολέμου. [online video]. http://www.avarchive.gr/portal/digitalview.jsp?get_ac_id=3895. Accessed on July 27, 2022.

Horton, A. (1999). *The films of Theo Angelopoulos: A cinema of contemplation* (3rd ed.). Princeton University Press.

Ioannopoulos, D. (1943). *The Voice of the Heart*. [film]. Finos Film.

Karalis, V. (2012). *A history of Greek cinema*. Continuum.

Kornetis, K. (2014). From reconciliation to vengeance: The Greek civil war on screen in Pantelis Voulgaris's a soul so deep and Kostas Charalambous's tied red thread. *Filmicon: Journal of Greek Film Studies*, 2, 93–116. https://filmiconjournal.com/journal/article/pdf/2014/2/6. Accessed on July 27, 2022.

Kranakis, M. (2015, July 13). Τα νησιά του ελληνικού σινεμά #13 – Η Μακρόνησος στο «Χάππυ Νταίη» του Παντελή Βούλγαρη. *Flix*. https://flix.gr/articles/greek-cinema-islands-happy-day.html. Accessed on July 27, 2022.

Margaritis, G. (2002). *Ιστορία του ελληνικού εμφυλίου πολέμου (τ. Α και Β)*. Vivliorama.

Mendrinos, A. (2021). Η ταινία ντοκουμέντο της Finos Film για την απελευθέρωση της Αθήνας – Ήταν απαγορευμένη κι αργότερα χαμένη για 55 χρόνια. *Newscenter.gr*. https://www.newscenter.gr/istoria-imeras/994832/h-tainia-ntokoymento-tis-finos-film-gia-tin-apeleytherosi-tis-athinas-itan-apagoreymeni-ki-argotera-chameni-gia-55-chronia/. Accessed on July 27, 2022.

Mixanitouxronou. (n.d.). "Ελένη". Η ταινία που αναζωπύρωσε τα εμφύλια πάθη…. https://www.mixanitouxronou.gr/quot-eleni-quot-i-tainia-poy-anazopyrose-ta-emfylia-pathi-oi-antidraseis-xekinisan-apo-tagyrismata-poy-telika-eginan-stin-ispania-eno-i-provoli-simadeytike-apo-epeisodia/. Accessed on July 27, 2022.

Mouratidis, P. (2009). *Εικόνες της ιστορίας: αποτυπώσεις και προσλήψεις της ιστορικής πραγματικότητας στο κινηματογραφικό έργο του Α. Σακελλάριου*. PhD Thesis. Department of History, Ionian Univesity. https://doi.org/10.12681/eadd/28265

Papadimitriou, L. (2005). *The Greek film musical: A critical and cultural history*. Mc Farland.

Psaras, T. (2018, January 11). Μια ταινία για μετά τον Εμφύλιο: Ο Τάσος Ψαρράς γράφει για το Καραβάν Σαράι. *Flix*. https://flix.gr/articles/caravan-serai-article.html. Accessed on July 27, 2022.

Richter, H. A. (2020). *Greece 1950–1974: Between democracy and dictatorship*. Harrassowitz.

Soldatos, Y. (1999). *Ιστορία του Ελληνικού Κινηματογράφου, τ. Β'*. Aigokeros.

Sotiropoulou, C. (1989). *Ελληνική κινηματογραφία 1965–1975: Θεσμικό πλαίσιο – Οικονομική κατάσταση*. Themelio.

Stamatopoulou, E. (2017). *Το νεοελληνικό θέατρο στα μεταπολεμικά χρόνια (1944–1967)*. PhD Thesis. School of Drama, Faculty of Fine Arts.

TVXS. (2011). Η αλήθεια για τα παιδιά της Ελλάδας. [online video]. https://www.dailymotion.com/video/xgt601. Accessed on July 27, 2022.

Valoukos, S. (2011). *Νέος Ελληνικός Κινηματογράφος: 1965–1981*. Aigokeros.

Vasilyev, G., & Vasilyev, S. (1934). *Chapaev*. [film]. Lenfilm.

Vidakis, G. (2021). Ντοκιμαντέρ – Η ΑΠΕΛΕΥΘΕΡΩΣΗ ΤΗΣ ΑΘΗΝΑΣ,12 Οκτωβρίου 1944 – ΦΙΝΟΣ ΦΙΛΜ. [online video]. https://www.youtube.com/watch?v=h6zSOl3_Us0&ab_channel=%CE%93%CE%B9%CF%8E%CF%81%CE%B3%CE%BF%CF%82%CE%92%CE%B9%CE%B4%CE%AC%CE%BA%CE%B7%CF%82. Accessed on July 27, 2022.

Voglis, P. (2006). Από τις κάννες στις κάμερες: ο Εμφύλιος στον ελληνικό κινηματογράφο. In F. Tomai (Ed.), *Αναπαραστάσεις του πολέμου* (pp. 103–122). Papazisis.

Zaharias, M. (2011). Αναμνήσεις μιας διαδρομής. Συνέντευξη. *Αρχειοτάξιο, 13*, 8–23.

Zervas, M. (2003). *Finos Film 1939–1977:* Ο *μύθος και η πραγματικότητα.* Agyra.

Zouboulakis, Y. (2011, June 5). Μια θρυλική συνοικία, μια καταραμένη ταινία. *To Vima.* https://www.tovima.gr/2011/06/05/culture/mia-thryliki-synoikia-mia-katarameni-tainia/. Accessed on July 27, 2022.

4

THIS WAR WILL BE EITHER TELEVISED OR TAPED: WWII IN THE GREEK DOMESTIC ENTERTAINMENT UNTIL THE DEREGULATION (1971–1989)

URSULA-HELEN KASSAVETI

Hellenic Open University, Greece

Keywords: Audiovisual deregulation; narrative film; VHS; historiography; digital history

INTRODUCTION: PLACING AND POPULARIZING HISTORY IN THE CONTEXT OF DOMESTIC ENTERTAINMENT

As a distinct historical period, World War II (WWII) has emerged as a recurring theme in cinema since its invention. Brave heroes, impossible battles, trauma, and dramatic implications have been central in various films, indifferent of origin, date, or style. Landy highlights that the historical film genre, which surfaced from WWII and onward, "often reveals the excesses of monumental history and its fascination with the spectacle and the heroic figure – embodied in stars who assumed the rich, famous, and powerful roles" (Landy, 2001, p. 8). In the following decades, history preoccupied different national arthouse or popular film cultures (to name a few): the 1920s and 1930s Russian pioneers, the Italian Neorealism of the 1940s, the 1950s historical films of Eastern Europe, the Italian peplum, or "sword-and-sandal" movies of the 1960s and blockbuster war films, such as *The Dirty Dozen* (Robert Aldrich, 1967) or *Where Eagles Dare* (Brian G. Hutton, 1968) to exploitation subgenres, such as "Macaroni Combat" or "Nampsloitation." The role of the film industry, the variety of cinematic approaches, and the uses of the cinematic past have shaped our viewpoint on the historical film – a generic term that seems to be culturally contested, as we will scrutinize below.

While cinema offers a different perspective on how history is perceived, processed, popularized, and manipulated by the respective filmmakers, the first thing to point out here is the difficulty of assessing the role of history in film. Historians and social scientists have generally adopted an ambiguous and skeptical attitude toward the cinematic representations of the past. From the polemics of François Amy de la Bretèque or Marc Ferro's view of how the past can be a valuable cinematic source (1988) to Rosenstone's argument on taking a critical standpoint on cinematic representations of war (Guynn, 2006, pp. 10–11), one cannot deny that history on film can become a privileged site for many, either naive or more insightful, interpretations.

Still, in the 20th and 21st centuries, much more attention has been directed toward history on film in contrast to television. Even with this somewhat visible play of analogy, history on television could also have gravity and urgency in understanding the past. The rise of television studies (Wheatley, 2008) and cultural studies with the novel analysis of narratives, production systems, and audiences make a concerted effort to evaluate and reassess certain television content and its association with a film. More recently, Mee and Walker (2014, p. 2) have argued how the two mediums interconnect, as, despite their differences, "it is undeniable that both film and television are ever-evolving, constantly embracing new forms and technologies and offering audiences new ways to watch – from the advent of home video in the late 1970s to more recent developments in the digital age" (Mee & Walker, 2014, p. 2). They contend that both cinema and television, particularly after the rise of "quality television," have shaped new perceptions of both media's older uses, i.e., with the advent of the World Wide Web and various on-demand film platforms.

As visual media have been paramount to our understanding of older or contemporary forms of culture, one should not exclude television as inferior to other mediatic forms. It reproduces some cinematic modes critically (Bignell, 2018, p. 264), transferring them to a domestic environment where choices, uses, and gratifications seem different. However, through its screen size, television transforms history and produces narratives that create a tight mesh of cultural and historical insights:

> *First, the motion picture, and then later its electronic offspring, television, became sometime during the 20th century the chief medium for carrying the stories our culture tells itself – be these*

set in the present or the past, be they factual, fictional, or a combination of the two. Blockbuster history films, mini-series, documentaries, docu-dramas, all these genres are increasingly crucial in our relationship to the past and our understanding of history. To leave them out of the equation when we think of the meaning of the past is to condemn ourselves to ignore the way a huge segment of the population has come to understand the event and the people who understand them. (Rosenstone, 2018, p. 3)

Along with television, video (video cassette recorder [VCR]) technologies also fall into the category of "domestic entertainment." The flourishing VCR market of the late 1970s and, in particular, the 1980s in the United States and Europe proposed a rather exciting alternative to film and television's technical and ideological ramifications. It empowered the viewers to choose what to watch – notably in countries such as Greece, where television was state-driven and freed the producers and the filmmakers from self-censorship.

This chapter centers on WWII narratives and representations in domestic entertainment (television and VHS) until the Greek audiovisual deregulation (1989). Choosing this particular time frame is crucial, as from the early advent of state television to its deregulation (1968–1989), the medium is held as a "negative allegory for modernization" (Paschalidis, 2018, p. 20). It was interconnected "with lots of sociocultural changes, such as – to name a few – the coup-d'-état and its effects on society and culture, the rise of consumerism, the turn to privatization, or the collapse of family values (Paschalidis, 2018, p. 20). A diachronic perspective follows the generic evolution of the Greek war television drama and addresses issues of fluidity, conservatism, and continuity with previous film formulas and conventions. Further, this chapter will explore another aspect of domestic entertainment: the direct-to-video films produced between 1985 and 1990, which investigate different and exciting aspects of WWII. Finally, it attaches importance to how this particular historical moment is represented on the small screen and how representational strategies perpetuate crystallized discourses about the war and the enemy through popular culture.

HISTORY REPRESENTED, HISTORY BIASED: EXISTING LITERATURE, PROBLEMS OF GENRE, AND METHODOLOGY

The interconnection between film and history has been further well-examined in Greek literature. Ever since Stassinopoulou's work (1995) on how history is embedded in Greek films until today, Greek cinema seems to have an exceptional gravity and urgency in offering popularized versions of historical events, such as the Greek Revolution of 1821 (see Dermentzopoulos, 2006; Kassaveti, 2021). The latter mainly refer to specific historical tensions in contemporary Greek history, such as the Macedonian Struggles, the Balkan Wars, and, to a limited extent, the Greek Civil War. For example, through a transnational examination in national cinemas, Lemonidou (2017) offers an interesting contribution to the role of film as an agent of public history. In the meantime, Andritsos emphasizes in his two studies (Andritsos, 2005, 2020) how WWII survived in different film genres and how it echoes in the lives of the films' characters. Andritsos's work aspires to extend to nonwar movies and re-engage a discussion of how the local film industry perceives the past and handles postwar trauma. After all, representations and discourses on war do not operate as "testimonies" (Andritsos, 2020, p. 57) but help us understand how Greek society received this conjecture. He contends that "what ultimately matters is not the views of historians on how the past should be represented in film but how, rightly or wrongly, filmmakers represent the past" (Andritsos, 2020, p. 60).

So far, Greek scholars have shed light on WWII representations in popular or arthouse Greek cinema. However, respective television fiction and direct-to-video films are fairly underexamined fields. The importance of other television genres, such as the soap opera or the comedy, has been adequately addressed (see Vamvakas & Gazi, 2017; Valoukos, 2008), while war serials/series have been marginalized. To this end, the popularity of such thematics during the 7-year military junta was thought to display a relation to the decade's dominant ideology. The latter has reasonably contributed to their obsolescence after the restoration of Democracy.

Furthermore, one should argue that the popularity of scriptwriter and director Nikos Foskolos's *Agnostos Polemos/Unknown War* (YENED, 1971–1974) had outshadowed most of the WWII television fiction ever produced for either state or private television. The same applies to the Greek direct-to-video circuit, which blossomed over 5 years, employing older popular genres and thematics. While many voice the critique that VHS films were cheap and rather kitsch cultural by-products, these direct-to-video ventures could offer a fascinating starting point on how the local audiovisual industry work and how older narratives (and narratives on history) can be encapsulated in a new format, which is in fact "new" only by name.

Considering all the constraints and tensions surrounding television and VHS war drama, this chapter will offer a new insight of how the genre works, survives, and further evolves (or not). To this end, it will adopt a historical – mainly drawing from Greek television history and VHS history – and a cultural standpoint, hailing from the politics of genre and cultural representation. To say, this is to suggest a shift of focus from theories that condemn "stated-related" television's ills to another "narrative." The latter is "broader and more culturally significant, as it focuses on large-scale cultural processes in which the popular is the critical arena for negotiating and shaping the new values and identities that accompany these processes" (Paschalidis, 2017, p. 45). Despite its marginality and being almost "invisible" (Aitaki, 2018, p. 201), Greek television culture may bring exciting aspects to the television genre and its discourses on society and history.

Based on quantitative and qualitative analysis, the following chapters begin with periodization and a brief overview of the war television drama genre and direct-to-video films exploring WWII until 1989. A further examination of the history and its representations will follow. Nevertheless, during the research, several problems arose. First, the sparsity of the audiovisual resources has been more than critical. While some archival material from the early days of state television has been salvaged, we access these shows through secondary sources, such as written memoirs from people who used to be old enough at the time of their screening or people who got involved in the first stages of organizing state television (Carter, 2004; Dampasis, 2002; Manthoulis, 1981). As many of these shows have been erased from their master tapes by the same people who had worked for the two state channels, we can only make assumptions about their content through bibliographical resources or trace some scenes via online video sharing and social media platforms, such as YouTube.

One problem worth noting was the genre per se, i.e., as a "means of managing TV's notorious extensiveness as a cultural form by breaking it up into more discrete or comprehensible segments" (Turner, 2004, p. 5). Operating on the triangle between media industry/text/audience and programmers, the television genre is a contested terrain if we consider issues of hybridity and overlapping. Steve Neale, who has exhaustively examined genre in cinema, poses the question:

What counts as a genre? What counts as a genre in television? Lacey (2000, p. 133) argues that the "repertoire of elements" that serve to identify genres consists of character types, setting, iconography, narrative, and style. This definition derives from, and seeks to encompass, popular fiction and films as well as television (Neale, 2004, pp. 3–4).

What is challenging, though, is how international-acclaimed television genres (such as soap operas or action adventures) are transcribed or "localized" by the vernacular media industry regarding production values and content. Considering that, it is tough to inscribe Greek war fiction within the

US and UK action series framework. According to Miller, these "focus on action rather than character, keeping with the medium's history and its social intertexts" (Miller, 2004, p. 17). They include "police programs, war shows that stress fighting over politics, and action-packed historical, science-fiction, espionage serials, off-beat buddy shows, cyborg/superhuman series, Westerns, and spoofs" (Miller, 2004, p. 17).

As we examine the genre within a local framework, Koukoutsaki offers another classification grounded on format, production mode, and broadcasting. Among "General drama," "Soap opera," and "Comedy drama," she adds "Adventure and crime drama" (Koukoutsaki, 2003, p. 720). As a further classification could be very "problematic," she contends that adventure and crime drama "is a category that covers a wide range of fiction dramas" with questionable distinctions among its subtypes. Koukoutsaki further pinpoints that such television dramas "lack sufficient budget, leading to indoor shooting and more dialogues" and a structure in "serial form" (Koukoutsaki, 2003, p. 721).

Not losing sight of this fact, we will examine the "action and drama" category as a generic fluid construction because, as we will ascertain later, war and its discourses on fiction film take another shape in contrast to its international counterparts.

Our sample consists of 14 serials/series and four direct-to-video films. In Table 4.1, one can ascertain the few serials revolving around WWII in contrast to the annual number of Greek television fiction of various genres (1971–1989).

Still, there was one more complication during the finalization of our sample. In particular, a small part of Greek television fiction partially involves WWII in its narratives, but not as a whole. For example, there are television serials/series covering an extensive period (e.g., 1920s–1950s decades) that do not constrain themselves only to WWII incidents. One can locate such examples in author Maria Iordanidou's biography serials *San Ta Trela Poulia/Like Crazy Birds* (ET1, 1987–1988) or *To Minore tis Avgis/Morning in Minor* (ERT, 1983–1984). Such serials dedicate only a few episodes that revolve around WWII, and sometimes (just in the case of *Minore*), the war is happening in the serials'/series' backdrop for only a short period. Therefore, they had to be excluded from our sample. Other serials, such as *I Zoi tou Attik/The Life of Attik* (ERT2, 1985–1986), occur during Midwar and WWII outbreaks in the last episode, such as in *Methysmeni Politeia/Drunken City* (ERT, 1980). They had, in turn, to be excluded from our sample, too.

Table 4.1. Production of WWII-Themed Greek Serials/Series (1971–1989) vs the Overall Production of Various Genres. All Entries Correspond to a Serial/Series' Seasons of Broadcasting. Therefore, They Should Not Be Counted as Single Entries.

Year	1971	1972	1973	1974	1975	1976	1977	1978	1979	1980	1981	1982	1983	1984	1985	1986	1987	1988	1989
WWII	2	2	4	4	1					1	3	1			3		2		1
Total	10	29	40	12	17	24	23	18	17	15	30	29	39	31	21	30	28	40	37

Source: Valoukos (2008); Retro.db.gr.

WWII FOR THE SMALL SCREEN: TRIUMPHANT, OVERDRAMATIC, AND ALMOST IMPOSSIBLE

The 1970s

The early days of Greek state television coincide with a crucial moment for the country, which has been under the Colonels' junta since 1967. While the new authoritative regime imposed censorship and opted for particular ethnocentric discourses in the vein of the "country, religion, and family" triptych (see Manthoulis, 1981, p. 34), television as a medium pervaded Greek domestic entertainment. Moreover, Greek television productions increased compared to American ones (Manthoulis, 1981, pp. 53–55). Despite the deficient audiovisual infrastructure, the 1970s is essential for the "understanding of social and cultural modernization of Greece" (Paschalidis, 2017, pp. 52–53). This period is further linked to the tremendous success of the *Agnostos Polemos/ Unknown War* serial, produced by Nikos Nikolareas, which marked the "last phase of dictatorial television, as its success is the trigger for the subsequent explosive development of Greek fiction" (Paschalidis, 2017, p. 53).

Agnostos Polemos, directed by both Kostas Koutsomytis and Nikos Foskolos, encapsulated several features recurring in the latter's films (Kassaveti, 2017a), such as the role of a doppelganger, the Greek intelligence service's heroic acts during WWII, and the complex plots. *Agnostos Polemos*'s basic narratives revolved around the war times and days of Colonel Diagoras Vartanis (Angelos Antonopoulos) and his brother-in-law, Captain Ektor Psahos (Kostas Karagiorgis). The latter's body double appears suddenly and strikes imbalance and additional complications for all the characters.

Valoukos mentions that the serial did not meet with success from its very moment, but after its second episode, its popularity took tremendous dimensions (Valoukos, 2008, pp. 68–69). In television critic Maria Papadopoulou's interview with Foskolos and in contrast to popular belief that he legitimized the junta through his television fiction, the scriptwriter and director had another viewpoint. He considered *Agnostos Polemos* "a constant pounding against fascism and totalitarianism and an anti-war series. For this reason, the audience loved it passionately. I refuse any other explanation" (Papadopoulou, 1975, p. 7). Foskolos insisted that he had adopted a particular historical viewpoint and tried to refrain from ambiguous discourses related to the Colonels' junta. He argued that "from the very first recording, I took down the picture frames of the dictator Ioannis Metaxas from the staff's offices! Three million viewers watched the serial for 2.5 years, and this initiative was not insignificant." Foskolos revealed that *Agnostos Polemos* was "a pure drama."

After the coup d'état of brigadier Dimitrios Ioannidis (1973), he was asked to move the plot from the African desert to Grammos. Foskolos refused, and since then, he had been unemployed until the 1990s (Papadopoulou, 1975, p. 7).

Overall, we must acknowledge that *Agnostos Polemos* was a television drama fashioned in a "period" iconography, merging war films with melodrama, and thriller. According to Paschalidis, the serial indicates the somewhat irregular political and cultural climate during the junta, and its impact on the audience was negligible (Paschalidis, 2013, pp. 54–59). *Agnostos Polemos*'s popularity in television and the blossoming production of war films in Greece led to the subsequent production of other war serials/series. Dampasis situates them in the context of the "embellishment of the military regime" (2002, p. 118), as producers involved in war films also occupy themselves with television productions. One example can be located in *I Proti Grammi*/*The First Line* (EIRT, 1971) series, produced by James Paris, the controversial film producer, and directed by Dimitris Papakonstantis (EIRT, 1971, p. 118). *I Proti Grammi* featured standalone episodes focusing on sergeant Grigoris Halkias (Giannis Katranis) and his battalion's acts of bravery, and it was based on *Combat*'s (ABC, 1962–1967) blueprint (Valoukos, 2008, p. 352).

Infused with elements of crime and espionage, the serial *Thisavroi tis Wehrmacht*/*Treasures of Wehrmacht* (YENED, 1972) was directed by Michalis Papanikolaou, a filmmaker with lots of experience in Greek state and, later, private television. Although the serial is set some years after WWII, it involves flashbacks of the actions of Wilhelm Kurt (Andreas Barkoulis), a Wehrmacht treasurer.

Marina Avgeri (EIRT, 1973) presents a fictitious portrait of a female university student fighting against the Nazis during the German Occupation. Actor Kostas Kazakos directed the serial, and his wife, Tzeni Karezi, played the role of Marina. Karezi provided the script under the alias "Pavlina Mpotasi."

Another instance of war drama is *Isidora* (EIRT, 1973–1974), the name of an Allies' operation and one of the protagonists. Film director Dimis Dadiras focused the serial on officer Apergis (Giannis Katranis). Using the alias "Vyron Tzavaras," he begins a quest under the orders of Middle East Command to kidnap German colonel Helmut Baumzer (Giorgos Moutsios), a specialist in flying bombs. When Tzavaras meets Helmut's wife, Isidora (Miranda Kounelaki), and falls in love with her, a weird mesh of conspiracies begins to unfold. Lastly, producer and advertiser Pavlos Pissanos carried out an ambitious approach to war drama with the serial *Katochi*/*Occupation*

(YENED, 1973–1974), which featured an all-star cast (Cürd Jurgens, Klaus Kinski, and others) (Dampasis, 2002, p. 134).

After the restoration of Democracy, the last war drama series *Polemikes Istories/War Stories* (YENED, 1974) is directed by Filippas Fylaktos. The filmmaker, known for his involvement in the 1960s Greek popular cinema, had directed war films, such as *Yperifanoi Aetoi/Proud Eagles* (1971) and *Pavlos Melas* (1974), and had been a long collaborator of the Greek Army. The series consisted of standalone episodes focusing on WWII, and these stories were the last to include war thematics at their core. The audience would have to wait until the next decade to watch war dramas again.

The 1980s

The Panhellenic Socialist Movement party's (PASOK) victory in 1981 sought to propose fundamental changes affecting Greek Society. In a quasi-socialist and rather populist spirit, PASOK intervened in how state television operated and attempted to transform its content in the vein of "Greekness" (Kassaveti, 2017c). That meant less screening time for foreign serials/series (and films) and more productions of Greek ones, infused by the spirit of *Allaghi* (The Change), PASOK's political project.

One year before Allaghi and almost 6 years after the last instance of the genre, a new war drama serial, *I Nychta/The Night* (ERT, 1980), was broadcast. The latter followed a woman that tried to save her family from hunger and the enemies during the German Occupation. Giorgos Skalenakis, an acclaimed Greek filmmaker, directed the serial, and actor Vassilis Andreopoulos, who had traumatic memories from WWII, wrote the script.

Book adaptations for the small screen, which had begun slowly in the previous period (Pappas, 2017), evolved as a popular strategy for television directors. As the new government took power in 1981, new series and serials were shot for Greek state television. In view of the above, war drama became under transformation as it pursued, in the meantime, to form into line with the new government's approach to culture. In 1981, the *Tragoudistades tis Lefterias/Singers of Freedom* (ERT, 1981–1982) serial was directed by veteran filmmaker Grigoris Grigoriou. A love drama set in WWII, *Tragoudistades*, was adapted from Giorgos Karageorgas's book of the same name, which had been popular since the late 1970s and had won the Greek Academy of Athens Award. *I Machi ton Pelargon/The Battle of the Storks* (YENED, 1981) was an adaptation of Notis K. Ryssianos's book and covered the Italo-Greek War, its battles (such in the Balkan peninsula), and the German Occupation. That was James Paris's last involvement with state television; the following year, he died.

In 1985, three serials revolving around WWII aired: *Kapnismenos Ouranos/Smoked Sky* (ERT2, 1985), directed by Kostas Koutsomytis, *Akybernytes Politeies/Drifting Cities* (ERT, 1985) by Roviros Manthoulis, and *I Eksafanisi tou Tzon Avlakioti/The Disappearance of John Avlakiotis* (ERT, 1985) by Errikos Andreou. The serials mentioned above share some standard features: all were directed by acclaimed filmmakers, are adaptations from well-known Greek books, and explore the limits of different genres, such as *Avlakiotis*, which had been the staple of crime literature by Giannis Maris. *Kapnismenos Ouranos* unfolds during the Greco-Italian War and the German Occupation, following different characters that try to survive during the war's challenging times. The serial had been an initiation to the small screen for old melodrama actress Martha Vourtsi, and each episode cost 2.000.000 drachmas. According to its director, Kostas Koutsomytis, "the characters are deeply human and are not uniquely limited to dealing with reality. They are hungry, in pain, in love, and passionate" (*Ta Nea, January 31, 1985, p. 8*).

Akybernites Politeies, a French–Greek–Israeli coproduction, also explored a mosaic of characters; yet, it is filmed and directed in a cinematic way and, in fact, interests itself more in the characters – victims or runaways from the war. The latter are located in Jerusalem (the shooting took place in Paris as well), and the serial focused more on their whereabouts and relationships than WWII – as it happens in Tsirkas's book. State television's ambitious effort to adapt the first part of the author's trilogy (*I Lesxi/The Club*) cost in toto 120 million drachmas (Ta Nea, January 11, 1985, p. 8) – a relatively inaccessible amount of money for any other director. The story follows second lieutenant Manos Symeonidis (Giorgos Coraffac), who escapes from the Greco-Italian War and finds shelter in the Middle East. He hides in a small cosmopolitan pension in Jerusalem – a tiny Babylon of all kinds of characters.

Finally, *I Exafanisi tou John Avlakioti* indicates state television's flirting with crime television fiction. An adaptation of Giannis Maris's (a.k.a. the "(grand)father of Greek crime fiction") iconic book, *I Exafanisi* begins in the Midwar and coincides with the beginning of the Greco-Italian War. Avlakiotis, a wealthy businessman, has gone missing, and his disappearance triggers a nightmarish chase between European spies and the German occupiers. According to *Avlakiotis*'s director, Errikos Andreou, "the serial has two levels: on the first level, it is a political espionage thriller, while on the second level, it tries to represent the heavy atmosphere of the Metaxas's dictatorship. Another element is the unusual romantic passion that dominates the myth. My effort focused on balancing all kinds of audiences into a 'single recipe'" (*Ta Nea tis Kyriakis*, April 21, 1985, p. 19).

Maria Dimadi (ERT2, 1987) was broadcast 2 years later and was directed by Giorgos Petridis. It portrayed Dimadi, a Greek heroine of the Resistance, whose life and work had been researched by Filippas Geladopoulos in his book (1982). Played by actress Eleni Saniou, Dimadi works as a translator in Agrinio's Kommandantur, where she educed critical information for the Greek Resistance. Her ceaseless and sacrificial activities led to her execution by the Germans.

Finally, *I Parelasi/The Parade* (ET1, 1989), directed by Giannis Diamantopoulos, marked the last of the war television drama examined. The serial takes place in Thessaloniki, where Tolis Kazantzis wrote the autobiographical novel *I Parelasi*. Actress Betty Valasi, already successful and famous for her role in the serial *Loxandra* (ERT, 1980), is "Mrs. Lisabet." Lisabet tries to support her four children during WWII, but as she is devastated by the circumstances exceeding her powers, she is compelled to leave Thessaloniki and find shelter and a better life in Athens.

The Direct-to-Video Films

From the early 1980s, VCRs enriched Greek domestic entertainment, offering an alternative to television spectatorship and cinema-going. In 5 years (1985–1990), a local direct-to-video circuit of various genres (ca. 1.116 video films) emerged on the premises of older actors, directors, and other agents of popular Greek cinema of older decades (Kassaveti, 2014, 2016). While it has been associated with allegedly hasty and rough production values and kitsch aesthetics, one must recognize the often humorous and on-point approach toward everyday life and its representations, as comments on society and politics infuse the video narratives.

In four instances, the Greek direct-to-video films adopt WWII as a relatively unexpected timestamp. One of the most interesting aspects surrounding WWII thematics is the return of Nikos Foskolos, who reshot *Agnostos Polemos* (1987) in two parts for the video market. The filmmaker had been almost "banned" from the Greek state television due to his former success of *Agnostos Polemos* and its association with the junta, and, jobless as he had been, his last resort was the local direct-to-video production (Delaportas, 2004, p. 126, pp. 128–129). He used the basic narrative plot from the old television serial and some actors from the first cast, such as Angelos Antonopoulos, who again played the role of Diagoras Vartanis. Nikos Apergis played the role of Ektor Psahos in the place of the deceased Kostas Karagiorgis, and Maria Aliferi took the place of Christina Psahou (initially played by Gkely Mavropoulou). This series of video films, broadcast as a mini television serial on the private channel of ANT1 in 1990, could serve as a small reconstruction of the television serial if someone had never watched it.

Foskolos's partnership with Elit video proved to be fruitful. Apart from *Agnostos*, his obsession with WWII took shape in another costly video production, *I Gynaika tis Protis Selidas/The Woman of the First Page* (1987), in three parts. He employed elements of older scripts with the body double as a staple of his plot. Zoe Laskari, a successful actress in popular Greek cinema, who had already collaborated with Foskolos, starred as Eugenia Christidi. Eugenia has survived the Nazi atrocities, but she is tortured by the memories of losing her only son after the experiments that Joseph Mengele carried out on her. Suffering from post-traumatic shock, she is enmeshed in further complications when a Jewish team tries to uncover a neo-nazist organization, where her body double owns an exceptionally high position. Although the video drama is set in the present, the ingenious Foskolos retouched how nazism craftily yet survives in modern societies.

In 1988, filmmaker Vangelis Fournistakis directed a peculiar direct-to-video music comedy starring the 1980s popular actress and dancer Eleni Filini. She is the *Kommandant Maria*, responsible for seducing Adolf Hitler during his stay in Athens. The video film is shot in a musical vein, but it does not belong to the musical film genre (see Kassaveti, 2017b). The songs and the places are profoundly modern, and the Hitler persona is rather sketchily represented, while the plot is outrageous. Still, it provides an example of a creative rendering of WWII.

Finally, in *Epta Mikroi Kommandos/Seven Little Commandos* (1988), Chris Sfetas, a miracle child in martial arts, plays the role of Chris, who saves a whole village from the Nazis and German commander Von Trichen (Ilias Konstantinou). As expected, the plot is excessively implausible. One does not expect that in the 1940s, a boy would be charged with the deliverance of a whole village. Giorgos Sfetas, Chris's father and a karate teacher, shot the video film to exemplify his son's martial art skills. Indicative of the impossible script is that 45 years after the end of WWII, Germans reoccupy Greece, and young children fight them, as the opening track notifies: "Neither our prayers nor the Army will save us/it is only the one and only, Chris the Terrible!"

WWII CONFLICTS AS CONFLICTS OF EMOTIONS: ALTERNATIVE VERSIONS OF HISTORY IN GREEK POPULAR CULTURE

The Greek war drama television serials/series and the direct-to-video films mentioned above offer some interesting insights regarding the interconnection between television, cinema, popular culture, genre, history, and ideology. Given the thematic continuities and shifts from the respective Greek 1970s war drama films, 1970s and 1980s war serials/series refrain from action sequences. Therefore, WWII is only a temporal marker and is used as a historical backdrop. In this sense, most television serials/series of the two decades disperse our concerns more widely across the characters than their actions (or the Resistance's), usually informed orally and not visually. Whether they stem from fiction (*Marina Avgeri*) or they are real people (*Maria Dimadi*), the female and male protagonists of television war drama are courageous, iconic, and "novelesque." They are more likely to represent the protagonists' internal conflicts in their quest to save their dignity and country. All characterizations are pushed to Manichean extremes when attributing traits to the enemy – may it be a German or an Italian. Women do have a fair share in the war of fiction. They are virtuous in a manner that they annihilate all their enemies – it is no surprise that almost all of the 1980s war serials/series are adaptations from novels, a common practice for television fiction after the Restoration of Democracy.

All the above utilize some of the same formal strategies and stylistic approaches that could be located in respective war drama films: close-ups for facial expressions, establishing shots for geographical indications, cliffhanging music, period costumes, and, predominantly, shooting in a studio. Shot-on-location is scarce, and when undertaken, it is associated with war missions of WWII. Television directors rally older newsreels to connect with the historical past to restore all plausibility and attain a documentary look. There is an ambivalence, though, surrounding how professionals tend to treat WWII. For instance, Roviros Manthoulis for *Akyvernites Politeies* undertook scrutinized research on academic books and the Greek politician Panagiotis Kanellopoulos's (one of the serials' main characters) archive (Golema, 1984, p. 8).

On the other hand, it is true that, despite their historical background, most serials/series were shot with the conventional treatment of the dramatic issues they sought to explore. They could be seen as agents of popularizing historical facts. Foskolos insisted that even when *Agnostos Polemos* "moves against the background of history, by its very nature it remains a drama and its dramatic characters are fatal to the whole scale of human emotions" (Papadopoulou, 1975, p. 7). For him, the serial had only been "a drama; it was not a history study. It operated on an established order" (Papadopoulou, 1975, p. 7). As for the allegiances that inscribe *Agnostos Polemos* in an intensely ideological climate, it is crucial to quote Giorgos Rallis, one of the most prominent radio and television producers of the 1970s: "If you undertook a psychological study, you would find out that [*AP*] left nothing, no residue in the audience. It did not civilize or educate – we agree on that. Nevertheless, it left nothing. It is gone" (Papadopoulou, 1974, p. 5).

Regarding 1980s VHS films, the rerelease of *Agnostos Polemos* on video with members of the old cast plus other actors and actresses is critical in understanding how Foskolos engaged in a strategy of filming and scriptwriting to present his obsession with WWII. Moreover, it is essential that this direct-to-video venture could reconstruct the old serial and could give a short glimpse to anyone who wanted to watch the serial in a new format. Notwithstanding Foskolos's ambitious endeavors, other direct-to-video films deviate from older popular war films. They seem to take advantage of the historical juncture to explore impossible and implausible plots, just like *Seven Little Commandos* and *Kommandant Maria*.

CONCLUSION

This chapter centered on WWII representations on Greek state television and the short-lived direct-to-video production (1985–1990) until the audiovisual deregulation of 1989. It argues that WWII television fiction, i.e., war drama, follows the pre-existing patterns of the respective film production, which gradually loses its interest in the war conflicts for the sake of emotional struggle. Despite the relative war iconography, serials and series of our sample are focused on rather atemporal subplots – highlighting the (melo)dramatic nature of the novels on which some were based – whose background is set loosely during WWII. Of course, this does not mean that the historical period per se does not affect the television characters who have to cope with the particular living circumstances of the Occupation. In the meantime, direct-to-video films seem at some point to deviate from the previous narratives (except for the restaging of *Agnostos Polemos*) and delve into a more paradoxical and humorous re-engagement of the particular historical period.

All previous concerns are bound up with the WWII representations examined in this chapter, so the genre is more flexible than expected. Thus, war television series/serials and, partially, direct-to-video films are close to period/costume drama. History is an agent of unfolding the main characters' dead ends while preserving a constrained view of Greek history. Notwithstanding these limitations, it is vital to remember Georges Sadoul's words:

> We should consider fiction films with no relation to particular historical events as historiographical sources. They have the same value as anything else that creative imagination produces, i.e., novel, drama, painting, etc. [...] They act as peerless treasures that interest history in general, but also the history of ethics, costume, gesture, the arts (which include cinema), of language, of technique. (Sadoul, 1988 [1961], pp. 21–22)

In this light, we should re-examine Greek war television fiction and direct-to-video films as creative products instances of historical fiction. Being undoubtedly products of the local popular culture, they simplified but simultaneously entertained the audience by offering some plausible (and, sometimes, rather implausible) instances of the Greek War of Resistance against the *Achsenmächte*.

REFERENCES

Aitaki, G. (2018). Aorati, mikri, politiki. I tileoptiki mythoplasia os (exostrefes) akadimaiko antikeimeno [Invisible, small, political. Television fiction as an (extrovert) academic discipline]. In V. Vamvakas & G. Paschalidis (Eds.), *50 hronia elliniki tileorasi [50 years of Greek television]* (pp. 197–212). Epikentro.

Andritsos, G. (2005). *I Katochi kai i Antistasi ston elliniko kinimatografo (1945–1966) [Occupation and resistance in Greek cinema (1945–1966)]*. Aigokeros.

Andritsos, G. (2020). *Kinimatografos kai istoria. I Katochi kai I Antistasi stis ellinikes tainies mythoplasias megalou mikous apo to 1945 mechri to 1981 [Cinema and history. Occupation and resistance in Greek full-length fiction films from 1945 to 1981]*. ΚΨΜ.

Bignell, J. (2018). Performing television history. *Critical Studies in Television: The International Journal of Television Studies, 13*(3), 262–279.

Carter, G. N. (2004). *Elliniki radiofonia tileorasi. Istoria kai istories [Greek radio and television. History and histories]*. Kastaniotis.

Dampasis, G. (2002). *Tin epohi tis tileorasis* [*At the times of television*]. Kastaniotis.

Delaportas, M. (2004). *O agnostos Nikos Foskolos* [*The unknown Nikos Foskolos*]. Orfeas.

Dermentzopoulos, C. (2006). Kinimatografos ke epanastasi. Anaparastaseis tis epanastasis tou 1821 ston elliniko kinimatografo eidon (1950–1975) [Cinema and revolution. Representations of 1821 in Greek genre cinema (1950–1975)]. In F. Tomai (Ed.), *Anaparastaseis tou polemou. I martyria tis kinimatografikis eikonas* [*War representations. The testimony of cinematic picture*] (pp. 239–253). Papazisi.

Ferro, M. (1988). *Cinema and history*. Wayne State University Press.

Golema, D. (1984, December 14). To akrivotero elliniko serial [The most expensive Greek serial]. *Ta Nea*, 8.

Guynn, W. (2006). *Writing history in film*. Routledge.

Kassaveti, O.-E. (2014). *I elliniki videotainia. Eidologikes, koinonikes kai politismikes diastaseis* [*The Greek direct-to-video film. Generic, social, and cultural dimensions*]. Asini.

Kassaveti, O.-E. (2016). Audiovisual consumption in the Greek VHS era: Social mobility, privatization and the VCR audiences in the 1980s. In K. Kornetis, E. Kotsovili, & N. Papadogiannis (Eds.), *Consumption and gender in southern Europe since the long 1960s* (pp. 241–256). Bloomsbury.

Kassaveti, O.-E. (2017a). *Antestrammena kosmoeidola. Dikastiko drama, melodrama, malakos erotiko kinimatografos (1966–1974)* [*Reversed worldviews. Courtroom drama, melodrama, softcore erotica (1966–1974)*]. Epikentro.

Kassaveti, O.-E. (2017b). From death to glory (?) and back again: Notes on the Greek popular film and direct-to-video musicals of the 1980s. *Filmicon*, *4*, 56–82.

Kassaveti, O.-E. (2017c). O sosialistikos eksamerikanismos tis ellinikis kratikis tileorasis kata tin periodo tis *Allaghis* (1981–1989) [The socialist americanization of Greek state television during the *Allaghi* (1981–1989)]. In V. Vamvakas & A. Gazi (Eds.), *Amerikanikes seires stin elliniki tileorasi. Dimofilis koultoura kai psychokoinoniki dynamiki*

[*American series on Greek television. Popular culture and psychosocial dynamics*] (pp. 141–180). Papazisi.

Kassaveti, O.-E. (2021). *1821: Ours, once more. When cinematic mythology creates history*. 23rd Documentary Film Festival Thessaloniki, Non/ Catalog (pp. 290–295). Nefeli.

Koukoutsaki, A. (2003). Greek television drama: Production policies and genre diversification. *Media, Culture & Society, 25*(6), 715–735.

Lacey, N. (2000). *Narrative and genre. Key concepts in media studies*. St. Martin's Press.

Landy, M. (2001). Introduction. In M. Landy (Ed.), *The historical film: History and memory in the media* (pp. 1–21). Rutgers.

Lemonidou, E. (2017). *I Istoria sti megali othoni. Istoria, kinimatografos kai ethnikes taftotites* [*History on the big screen. History, cinema, and national identities*]. Taksideftis.

Manthoulis, R. (1981). *To kratos tis tileorasis* [*The state of television*]. Themelio.

Mee, L., & Walker, J. (2014). Introduction. Cinema, television and history. In L. Mee & J. Walker (Eds.), *Cinema, television and history: New approaches* (pp. 1–11). Cambridge Scholars.

Miller, T. (2004). The action series. In G. Creeber (Ed.), *The television genre book* (pp. 17–18). BFI.

Neale, S. (2004). Genre and television. In G. Creeber (Ed.), *The television genre book* (pp. 3–4). BFI.

Papadopoulou, M. (1974, July 8). To fiasco ton serials: Giorgos Rallis [The fiasco of serials: George Rallis]. *Ta Nea*, 5.

Papadopoulou, M. (1975, July 9). To fiasco ton serials: Nikos Foskolos "I Hounta itan i megalyteri thavmastria mou" [The fiasco of serials: Nikos Foskolos 'Junta had been my greatest fan']. *Ta Nea*, 7.

Pappas, F. (2017). Proti metapoliteytiki periodos (1974–1981): Epelasi tis tileorasis, pagiosi tis amerikanikis tileoptikis psychagogias kai prospatheia eghoriou-poiotikou antistathmismatos [First period after the restoration of democracy (1974–1981): Emergence of television, consolidation of american television entertainment and attempt at local quality counterpoint]. In V. Vamvakas & A. Gazi (Eds.), *Amerikanikes seires stin elliniki tileorasi. Dimofilis koultoura kai psychokoinoniki dynamiki*

[*American series on Greek television. Popular culture and psychosocial dynamics*] (pp. 103–140). Papazisi.

Paschalidis, G. (2013). Entertaining the colonels: Propaganda, social change and entertainment in Greek television fiction, 1967–74. In P. Goddard (Ed.), *Popular television in authoritarian Europe* (pp. 53–70). Manchester University Press.

Paschalidis, G. (2017). Tileoptiki psychagogia 1967–1974: Ta amerikanika afigimata syneheias [Television entertainment 1967–1974: American television narratives]. In V. Vamvakas & A. Gazi (Eds.), *Amerikanikes seires stin elliniki tileorasi. Dimofilis koultoura kai psychokoinoniki dynamiki* [*American series on Greek television. Popular culture and psychosocial dynamics*] (pp. 41–102). Papazisi.

Paschalidis, G. (2018). Eisagogi [Introduction]. In V. Vamvakas & G. Paschalidis (Eds.), *50 hronia elliniki tileorasi* [*50 years of Greek television*] (pp. 9–41). Epikentro.

Rosenstone, R. A. (2018). *History on film/film on history*. Routledge.

Sadoul, G. (1988). Fotografia kai kinimatografos [Photography and cinema]. In C. Samaran (Ed.), *Istoria kai oi methodoi tis (tomos b'). Methodiki anazitisi ton martyrion* [*L' Histoire et ses Méthodes*] (pp. 11–26). MIET.

Stassinopoulou, M. (1995). Ti gyrevei i istoria ston kinimatografo? [What is history seeking in the movies?]. *Ta Istorika, 12*(23), 421–423.

Turner, G. (2004). The genre and its limitations. In G. Creeber (Ed.), *The television genre book* (pp. 4–5). BFI.

Valoukos, S. (2008). *Istoria tis ellinikis tileorasis* [*History of Greek television*]. Aigokeros.

Vamvakas, V., & Gazi, A. (Eds.). (2017). *Amerikanikes seires stin elliniki tileorasi. Dimofilis koultoura kai psychokoinoniki dynamiki*. Papazisi.

Wheatley, H. (Ed.). (2008). *Re-viewing television history: Critical issues in television historiography*. I. B. Tauris.

5

GERMAN CONQUERORS IN THE GREEK FULL-LENGTH FICTION FILMS FROM 1945 TO 1981

YIORGOS ANDRITSOS

Independent Researcher, Greece

Keywords: Greek cinema; German occupation; postwar films; historical representation; cultural memory

INTRODUCTION

In this chapter, we attempt to detect the manner of presentation of the German conquerors in the Greek fiction films from 1945 to 1981. We dealt with these films as their era testimonies and tried to link them with the frame in which they were created, by correlating the film speech evolution with the social, political, and cultural developments. Our interest is the image films create, and what purpose this creation serves. Films interpret national history for the broad public and thus produce, organize and, to a large extent, homogenize public memory. Before the advent of television, cinema was the most effective vehicle for shaping historical consciousness (Anton Kaes, 1990, p. 112). Films exert an enormous influence over the shaping of popular historical understanding and provide spectators with images which, very often, substitute for actual memories, creating a contrived but very effective idea for the past (Sorlin, 1999, p. 107).

The films were not studied as works of art. The films which considered being of a better artistic value aren't discussed here in more depth, as films that considered having a poorer quality, in many cases, were big successes in the box office (Heartney, 2002). Films of the so-called popular cinema were analyzed. Even those which were lacking in technical perfection because to quote Vitkenstein, "we can earn a valuable lesson from a stupid movie" (Virilio, 2005, p. 15). While many films are variations of the same theme, they were all studied as none is identical to another, and each one can contribute valuable elements/information (Dudley, 1998, p. 177) to the analysis.

We studied the way in which the German conquerors are represented in these films and tried to detect the changes in the way of representation during the examined period and the changes that took place in the Greek society and the international sociopolitical framework. Finally, we attempted to answer the difficult question of how the audiences perceived the films, combining the box office figures, their reception by critics of selected newspapers from the entire political spectrum as well as of cinema magazines, but also the public reactions that often resulted from some of these films. We have distinguished three big periods based on the social and political developments in Greece. The first starts with the liberation from the Germans and ends with the imposing of the dictatorship. The second starts from the coup and ends with the fall of the junta. The third covers the period from the reestablishment of democracy to the prevalence of PASOK in the 1981 elections.

The main queries that occupied us are: Are there any periods that they are mentioned more frequently and others that they are seldom referred to? In what aspects with the passing of time are differentiations observed, and in what aspects the representation remains constant?

EXPLORING THE REPRESENTATION OF GERMAN CONQUERORS: THE FILMS

The representation of Germans in the Greek films begins with the film *Raid in the Aegean* (1945) by the well-known author M. Karagatsis. The Germans are represented as cruel, inhuman, but even if their military abilities are recognized, they are rather "naïve," as the saboteurs, "[...] meet mainly stupefied Germans, in front of which they perform thousands of naïve deeds, without not a clever German but a pair of eyes that can see properly to be found [...]" (Pellico, 1947, pp. 3–4).

In the film *Unconquered Slaves* (1946) by Vionas Papamichalis, the Germans subject members of the Resistance to horrible tortures in Merlin and Haidari, while they executed in cold blood a 6-year-old child. In *The Last Mission* (1948) by Nikos Tsiforos, next to the inhuman and cynical officers that sadistically torture the members of the Resistance, we have the likeable portrayal of a soldier, who is presented as a victim of war. However, he is not a German but an Austrian, a fact that explains in a big extent why he is presented differently in the film. In *Bloody Christmas* (1951) by Giorgos Zervos, we have a likeable portrayal of soldiers who desire to return to their country because they are sick of war, simultaneously to the usual presentation of the Germans. In *The Barefoot Battalion* (1953) by Greg Talas, we have a likeable presentation of a German officer.

In *Bitter Bread* (1951) by Grigoris Gregoriou, the Greek Jews persecution by the Germans, which led to the devastation of the Jew communities of Greece, is presented for the first time. This film is about the story of a Jew who survived the concentration camps, in which his family was "wiped out." In *The Knights' Tower* (1952) by Giorgos Asimakopoulos and Nikos Tsiforos, a reference to the Greek Jews' persecution is also made. In the films *The Flame of Freedom* (1951) by Panagiotis Spyrou, *We Remained Two of Six* (1952) by Stavros Hatzopoulos, and the *Return from the Front* (1958), the Germans advance to mass retaliation and execute civilian population. In the second film, extended references to starvation are made, for which the Germans are responsible because "they are infuriated about the heroic resistance and grab all consumables," while they shoot at children that "jump on trucks to steal a loaf of bread."

Three different representations of the Germans are observed in *The Island of the Brave* (1959a). The Germans burn down the houses and execute a whole village's population, when they refuse to reveal where the partisans are hiding. An inhuman officer of the Schutzstaffel (SS; German for protective echelon) stands out among them, who also "likes the Greeks and has lived in Greece in the past." The portrayal of a career officer (played by Lykourgos Kallergis) of the German army is different. When he finds out that the woman he loves has stolen classified military information from him, he feels betrayed, but he does not react violently. Finally, he bravely commits suicide, paying the penalty of losing the documents. A mere soldier is portrayed in a highly elaborate description. In the sabotage scene, he treats a girl who is pretending to be a prostitute, trying to distract him kindly. He says to her: "I do not like killing. I want to go back home." When he meets her again, he lets her go, although he recognizes her. He characteristically says: "You should have killed me. English soldiers demolished my house. They are all dead" and he wonders: "Why should there be a war?" He is the simple man who got carried away by the maelstrom of the big events and got involved in the insanity of war.

Kostas Stamatiou praised the film and associated it with the bill about the amnesty of war criminals: "[...] execution of innocent people from Hitler followers, villages burning, guerillas retaliations, sabotages, ambushes, pursuits [...] the Hitler followers (who speak german when they must) you feel are real Germans [...]. The timeliness of the theme that was aroused by the voting of the bill for amnesty to the war criminals, was proved by last night's reactions of the first viewers, general emotion, national pride that were spontaneously expressed with applauses in every 'strong' scene [...]" (October 27, 1959a).

In the film *Soldiers without a Uniform* (1959b) by Dimitris Ioannopoulos, a German kills a child who stole a tin can, while in the melodrama *Our Tears have Dried Out* (1961) by Giorgos Papakostas, a German kills a child who was selling cigarettes. In *The Dawn of Triumph* (1960) by Filippos Fylaktos, the Germans execute people in retaliation of the saboteurs' actions. However, we have the likeable portrayal of a German officer. He punishes mercilessly the woman he loved because she attempted to steal valuable documents, but after his action, grief-stricken, he asks to return to the "abattoir" of the eastern front, a decision that equals suicide. Kostas Stamatiou commented acidly: "[...] the main German hero of the film is an amiable "gentleman" who declares that he hates war, while the Greeks declare that "they who sabotage are responsible for the retaliations [...] the Germans themselves have filmed more anti-Nazi films[...]" (October 27, 1959b).

The *Stick your Hands up Hitler!* (1961) by Roviros Manthoulis concentrated a German officer who is having a picture taken with Acropolis in the background, while a soldier is kicking away the protagonist (played by Thanasis Veggos), who is getting in the way. Here, we have reference on the Germans' love for the classical years as opposed to the cruelty toward the occupied Greeks. In the film *The Siege* (1962) by Claude Bernard Auber, the Germans burn down a village, rape women, and kill civilian population. In the film *They Hide our Sun* (1963) by Thanasis Santas, we have the execution of 40 men for the murders of two low rank officers, while a German shoots in cold blood a young man who was writing political slogans on a wall.

The story of a German officer (played by Zoras Tsapelis) who had a leading role in the persecution of the Jews of Salonika and returns to Greece years later searching for a hidden treasure is presented in the film *Amok* (1963), by Dinos Dimopoulos. The film brings up the issue of the impunity of war criminals, referring to the "Merten Case," which had upset Greece and had caused intense political confrontation. Max Merten, although sentenced for 25 years imprisonment, was deported to West Germany after two and a half years in jail, on November 5, 1959, because he was reportedly keeping information about members of the Karamanlis government behavior during the German occupation (Fleischer, 1995, vol. 2, p. 326.). The magazine *Art Review* commented acidly: "[...] As a height peak, a national hero of the stature of Manolis Glezos is arrested for conducting espionage [...] while executioners of Greek people, like the infamous Merten are set free [...]" (Art Review, 1958, pp. 4–6). References about the Greek Jews persecutions are found also in the films *Brother Anna* (1963) by Grigoris Gregoriou, *The Misconduct of an Orphan* (1963) by Avgoustos Sklavos, and *To Be or Not to Be?* (1965) by Orestis Laskos.

Another representation of a German Officer is provided in the film *Misconduct of an Orphan*, where a mysterious German officer collaborates with a Resistance group and transfers valuable information in the allies' headquarters in the Middle East. *The betrayal* (1964), directed by Kostas Manousakis, and Aris Alexandrou's screenplay, begins with a tragic romantic story between a German officer and a Greek Jew woman, making extended references to the German atrocities in the concentration camps. The officer (played by Petros Fyssoun) has all those qualities that make him amiable. He is educated, having a passion for music, he is gentle; thus, his betrayal of his beloved one causes a bigger shock to the viewer. The film condemns the fascist ideas that caused bloodshed around the planet and points out the dynamics of fascism on the wider population masses, particularly the youth. Antonis Moschovakis praised the film: "[...] The protagonist, a German officer, young, pure, emotional, realizes after a series of dramatic events that he is a ruthless criminal for letting his soul to be poisoned by the disastrous Nazi delusion, this beastly ideology [...]" (November 24, 1964). The film represented Greece in the Cannes festival and received negative reviews by the French cinema critics, who blamed the director for the extended use of Nazi ceremonies and scenes from the Triumph of Will (1934) by Leni Riefenstahl, claiming that he unwillingly preserves the image of the Nazi party greatness, which cinematographers collaborating with the Nazi regime had so capably constructed (The Postman, 1966).

In the film *When the Bells Toll* (1964) by Stelios Tatasopoulos, the Germans burn down a village and kill civilian population running for their lives. In the melodrama *My Life Belongs to You* (1965) by Panagiotis Konstantinou, the Germans torture a pregnant woman to get information from her. In the film *Forgotten Heroes* (1966) by Nikos Gardelis, an officer attempts to rape a young woman who is asking about her imprisoned brother. The film *The Round-Up* (1965) by Adonis Kyrou transfers onto the big screen the Kokkinia round-up, that took place on the August 17, 1944, where the Germans and members of the German-armed "security battalions" executed 150 members of EAM (National Liberation Front) and took thousands of prisoners in the Haidari prison. Antonis Moschovakis pointed out that "[...] It authentically presents the German occupation, the barbarous behavior of the occupants [...]" (September 28, 1965). In the film *The Traitor* (1966) by Ilias Macheras, there is a reference to the Kesariani and Vyronas round-ups on the April 21, 1944, while in the melodrama *The Brothers* (1966) by Kostas Doukas, we have a reference on the Kallithea round-up on the July 23, 1944 (Grigoriadis, pp. 140, 332).

In 1966, Panos Glykofrydis concentrated on the execution of 30 men in a village, in retaliation of the murder of a German soldier, in the film *With Shine in the Eyes*. The film focuses on a father's dilemma, who is asked by the Germans to choose one of his three children to be executed. In the German officer's (played by Zoras Tsapelis) speech, we have a reference on the fascist ideology, when he pinpoints that "[....] the national socialist soldier fights to save Europe from Bolshevism and Communism [...]" (Hobsbawm, 1991, p. 157). Antonis Moschovakis, although having praised the film, claimed that: "[...] The hideous murder of a German soldier in an unmanly way (a tired man gets a shot in the back while drinking water), is opposed to reality and is an aesthetic contradiction in the film. The resistance – evaluating the consequences – never sniped against Germans (only traitors) [...]" and accused the director that "[...] in a way he excuses the beasty retaliations of the Germans [...]" (September 27, 1966).

In the film *The Young Want to Live* (1964) by Nikos Tzimas, the protagonist, forced by poverty, is going to Germany to work for those who "hanged" his father who participated in the Resistance. In the film *The Enemies* (1965) by Dinos Dimopoulos, the main character who was left lame by a German's bullet during the occupation hates everything that is German but emigrated to Germany, while in the film *Face to Face* (1966) by Roviros Manthoulis, emigrants attend German language lessons and stamp their passports in order to contribute to the "German Miracle" and a voice over comments: "Ah! Greek food, how many Germans have you fed!" and a sign written in German appears on the screen reading: "German soldier, do not offer your food to the Greeks, because they will strengthen and will hit you!" The films echoed the hostility toward Germany, as the wounds from the occupation period were still open and the German atrocities were not forgotten. The disasters the occupation caused are related to the drain of the most productive part of the population and its exploitation from West Germany in the postwar era. In 1958, the number of Greek workers in Germany was only 3.000, while in 1969 reached to 300.000 (Psyroukis, 1975, p. 183).

The references to the German occupants increased during the dictatorship. In the films: *The thirteenth* (1967), *The Mediterranean is Burning* (1969), and *NO* (1969) by Dimis Dadiras, *Bread for a Fugitive* (1967) and *There are no*

Deserters (1970) by Kostas Asimakopoulos, *Gorgopotamos* (1968) and *Grammos* (1971) by Ilias Machairas, *Afrodite, The Girl That Got Hurt* (1968) by Giorgos Lois, *The Teacher With the Blond Hair* (1969) by Dinos Dimopoulos, and *The Last Prisoner* (1970) by Aggelos Georgiadis, there are extended references about German mopping-up operations and executions of civilian population in retaliation to the partisans operations. In the film *Haidari, Time: 3:30, Escape!* (1967) by Ilias Machairas, a sadist officer has his photograph taken with a prisoner and says: "When I execute you, I will hang your shirt on my uniform, along with the Polish doctor and the ballerina from Prague." In the films *Times of Love, Times of War* (1969) by Antonis Tempos, *Those who Spoke with Death* (1969) by Giannis Dalianidis, and *Guerillas of the Cities* (1971) by Dimis Dadiras, German officers are presented as common blackmailers. They extract money from prisoners' relatives by "selling false hopes," promising to save them. As mentioned in the *Guerillas of the Cities*: "Pigs sell out their own mother for gold."

Focusing on a critical comment for the impunity of German criminals of war, three Germans return to Greece looking for a hidden treasure, in the film *An Incredible Sucker* (1968) by Thanasis Veggos. In the melodrama *A wreck of Life* (1968) by Giorgos Papakostas, there is an extended reference to the persecution of the Jews of Athens. References to the Greek Jews' persecutions have come across in the films *The Traitor Must Die* (1970) by Errikos Andreou and in *Flamed Bodies in Sin's Vertigo* (1972) by Pavlos Paraschakis, while in the films *On High Treason* (1968) by Thanasis Papageorgiou, *Mr Station Master* (1971) by Dimitris Bazaios, and *The Years of Wrath* (1972) by Christos Kyriakopoulos, there are references to the eliminations of Jews in the concentration camps.

Kostas Karagiannis in the film *October 28, 5:30* (1970) focused on German soldiers who hesitate to shoot a man, crippled on the Albanian front, when he tears up a swastika flag. The soldier who refuses to shoot gets shot by a sadist SS officer (played by Lakis Komninos), who goes on and kills the crippled man in cold blood. The dictatorship supporting morning newspaper: *The New State*, asked for the scene "[...] where the hero's father arrests the village's German officer in command and attempts to cut off his legs with an axe, because his hero son had lost both his legs on the Albanian front" to be removed. Although he finally gets hold of himself "the thought of such an atrocity is offensive to the Greek fighters, who always claim their freedom with heroic deeds, manly and brave, but not barbarous" [...] (Tsirbinos, 1971).

In the early 1970s, women fighters illustrate the superiority of Greeks over the Germans, based on the glorious past and the achievements of the ancient Greek civilization in two films, *The Fortress of the Immortals* (1970) by John

Christian and *The Dawn of Victory* (1971) by Dimis Dadiras. In the first example, a female partisan imposingly answers an officer's indication that "Hitler wants to create a new civilization. It is your poor mind that does not get our intentions," that "Civilization was created by us long before Hitler." In the second example, a female partisan dumbfounded an officer: "For entire centuries, people of this land have never changed their minds. From the times people of your world lived in caves, while people of our world had discovered the human spirit. These are not my words, but your leader's."

A different representation, which focuses on a positive portrayal of the Wermacht carrier officers (played by Giorgos Kampanellis and Lykourgos Kallergis respectively), is provided in the films *The Canon and the Nightingale* (1968) by Giorgos and Iakovos Kampanellis and *The Fortress of the Immortals*. In a similar approach, focusing on conscience, there are two cases in which German soldiers are represented as committing suicide. In the first example, an officer (played by Aggelos Antonopoulos), who had a leading contribution to the massacre of Kalavryta, commits suicide as he feels guilty (*A German in Kalavryta Town*, 1970, by Memas Papadatos). In the second example, in the *Lieutenant Natasha* (1970) by Nikos Foskolos, an SS officer (played by Kostas Karras) commits suicide when he finds out that his mother is a member of the Resistance.

Focusing on anti-fascism, *Death Mission* (1968) by Marios Retsilas concentrated on a mysterious anti-fascist officer who gives valuable information to the members of the Resistance of which the woman he loves is also a member and later he sacrifices himself to prevent her arrest. He calls the officer who arrests him "a Hitlerian pig," while he accuses Hitler of the war's devastation: "[...] why is it that this war should be happening? A war that started off by a man's ambition to end up in the death of millions of others [...]," following the widespread nonscientific perception which incriminated Hitler as the only responsible for all Nazi crimes (Elsaesser, 1996, pp. 156–157).

IN THE FILM

An extraordinary portrayal of a common German soldier (played by Antonis Papadopoulos), who gets trapped in the maelstrom of events and tries to survive, preserving his humane behavior, is presented in 1971, in *What Did You Do in the War, Thanasis?* (1971) by Dinos Katsouridis. He is the victim of the events, and he breathes his last, tortured by his compatriots, as he covers up for his Greek friend. In the film *Holocaust* (1971) by Dimitris Papakonstantis, a soldier (played by Christos Politis) hates Germans and accuses Hitler of calling up 12-year-old children to serve in the armed forces. Although he gets heavily wounded by the partisans, he sacrifices himself to save the children the Germans try to abduct, in retaliation to the killings of five soldiers. Vasilis Rafailidis commented ironically: "[...] The Austrian, who is the good of the film, (speaks Greek as well) he is proclaimed Austrian, due to our deeply rooted racist idea that all Germans are born bad [...]" (1971, p. 12).

Focusing on the Kalavryta massacre, which took place on December 13, 1943 and considered being one of the biggest German atrocities in Greece, in the film *A German in Kalavryta Town*, we get an insight into the Greek governments' attitude, who were indifferent to war criminals' persecutions, giving priority to the good relations with West Germany and yielding to its economic threatening (Fleischer, 2003–2004, p. 21). "The slayer of Crete was given back to his own people, so that the German market that bought our tobacco would not get displeased. The same happened with Merten, the same is going to happen now. They will give away Kruger for the tobacco, the oranges [...]."

After the fall of the dictatorship, the references to the German conquerors are reduced. In the films *In the Nets of Terror* (1974) by Dimis Dadiras, *The Hunters* (1977) by Theodoros Angelopoulos, *The Bald Student* (1979) by Dinos Katsouridis, and *A Laughing Afternoon* (1979) by Andreas Thomopoulos, there are some references to the Germans, while in the films *Isidora* (1974) by Dimis Dadiras, *The Mad Kamikazi* (1980) by Dinos Katsouridis, *Seventeen Bullets for an Angel* (1980) by Takis Vougiouklakis, and *Educate Yourself My Child* (1981) by Thodoros Maragkos, executions of civilian people in retaliation to the guerillas' operations are presented. In the film *The Travelling Players* (1975) by Theodoros Angelopoulos and in *The Man with the Carnation* (1980) by Nikos Tzimas, the Germans' crimes of war are directly related to the Nazi ideology. In the film *Seventeen Bullets for an Angel*, a German officer is being bribed to let the imprisoned heroin escape. In the film *Agent Nelie* (1981) by Takis Vougiouklakis, there is an extended reference to the German Jews' persecutions after Hitler came to power. In the films *Isidora* and *Agent Nelie*, we came across the contrivance of the German double agent. In the first, a German woman pretends to be a Jew who lost her parents in a concentration camp and causes big damage to the Resistance, while in the second, an SS officer (played by Phaedon Georgitsis) pretends to be an English anti-fascist and achieves the breaking up a major Resistance group.

The Big Canon (1981) by Panos Glykofrydis brings up the issue of the neo-Nazism reappearance and its effects to young people. It stresses the need for the Nazi crimes not to be forgotten so as to prevent them from appearing again in the future. The issue was – and still is – in the news, since neo-Nazists made their presence noticeable with bomb explosions and beatings of leftist people (*The Dawn*, 1978a, 1978b). The protagonist (played by Thanasis Veggos) says resentfully to his neo-Nazi son: "Have they told you about the occupation? [...] for the children that were starving to death, and we were collecting them from the streets to throw them in the garbage as if they were dogs. For your father, me, who was a dragsman, and that when Frietz caught me stealing an army bread he broke my arm on his knee [...]."

CONCLUDING REMARKS

The Germans have the lion's share in the Greek films about the occupation, that were filmed between 1945 and 1981. Their leading role is justified, as they defeated the Greek army and had the last word on issues concerning occupation in Greece. They had control of the three big cities, and after the collapse of the Mussolini regime, in 1943, they replaced the Italians in the whole country (Papastratis, 1984, pp. 113–114). The Germans, with a few exceptions, are represented as cruel and inhuman. They submit prisoners to horrible tortures; they execute civilian people and kill in cold blood, even little children. Although most films recognize the military ability and organization of the Germans, the saboteurs achieve the most incredible deeds "under their very nose." Scenes of action in many films reach the limits of "ludicrousness" as the saboteurs overpower the Germans in a "magic" way (Sorlin, 1980, p. 200).

In several films, we repeatedly see the differentiation of the "immaculate" Wermacht regular army and its exoneration of war crimes, which were exclusively attributed to the SS. That was one of the most enduring myths in German history, in the creation of which, the most films created in Western Europe and the United States contributed decisively. It is only in the recent years that this myth is being disputed (Fleischer, 2003, p. 57). It is worthwhile underlining the paradox of the different approach to the Austrians, although two of them, Hermann Neubacher and Alexander Lohr, were governing Greece in September 1943 (Mazower, 1994, p. 250). This different approach is due to the postwar exoneration of the Austrians for their Nazi past. They were included in the victims' side, although Germany annexed Austria in 1938, without any military Resistance, while National Socialism gained great power in the country (Hobsbawm, 1991, p. 191).

In two films, we have Germans collaborating with the Resistance. These films maybe reminded the audience the German anti-fascists who gave information and arms to the Resistance while indeed quite a few of them joined Ελληνικός Λαϊκός Απελευθερωτικός Στρατός (ELAS; Greek for Greek peoples' Liberation Army). It is mainly about the disciplinary battalions of 999 soldiers, who were sent to Greece in 1943. In the summer of 1944, 600 Germans were fighting for Ελληνικός Λαϊκός Απελευθερωτικός Στρατός (ELAS; Greek for Greek peoples' Liberation Army). Overall, about 1,000 German soldiers, mostly communists, defected to the ELAS (Eberchard, 2007, pp. 71–78). However, there are differentiations in the Germans' portrayal as time passed. The films created until 1948 present Germans with the darkest colors and focus on their crimes. After the cold war started, the number of films about the occupation is reduced, and German crimes are suppressed. In the cold war situation, Nazi crimes were deliberately degraded because they were causing problems to the North Atlantic Treaty Organization (NATO). The Germans were not enemies anymore, but valuable allies against the new enemy, the "Soviet Totalitarianism" (Novick, 1999). In 1948, Panagiotis Pipinelis, a chairman to the board of political affairs of the Greek government, pointed out "[...] to the interest of the entire Europe, in general, and of Greece in particular, Germany – the country that committed crimes against our country – has to be reconstructed [...] In this effort, it is in our interest to help them, within our power limits" (Fleischer, 2009, pp. 527–528).

On top of that, in 1952, the ministry of external affairs pointed out that "[...] the German ambassador drew our attention to the unfortunate recent impact a greek film made, showing scenes from the german occupation in Greece[...]." reporting that "[...] a fierce anti greek article was published because of this film, in a german comics magazine [...]" and suggested to evaluate "[...] as to how it would be possible for this film to be withdrawn from distribution or at least for future avoidance of producing such films," as "it is necessary to the greek interests, to stop stirring up the past [...]," because "[...] we already have great commercial interests in Germany which get damaged[...]" and "[...] we already look forward to the german cooperation with the democratic countries group for the sake of Europe's defense[...]" (National Archives).

When Konrad Adenauer visited Athens in 1954, the Prime Minister Alexandros Papago praised "Free Germany," while Adenauer convicted the "devastating past," praised the Greek people's Resistance to the "totalitarian states during the war, and later to communism," and he laid "a laurel wreath at the German soldiers' graves that died in Greece" (Linardatos, 1977, p. 152). In 1959, the government let free the war criminal Hans Gunther Kolwes because, as the minister to the president Kostantinos Tsatsos stated, "the politics toward the ending of the war criminals persecution is in accordance to the broader interests of the country" (Linardatos, 1977, pp. 458–460). This situation started taking a turn in the late 1950s, with films referring to German mopping up operations, tortures, and massive executions. The West Germany embassy was annoyed by these films which portrayed Germans "as scum, almost without an exception" and contained torture scenes and executions. The ambassador Gebhard Seelos pointed out on the October 29, 1959, referring to the film *The Island of the Brave*, that films that "[...] bring back an unpleasant past to the viewers' consciousness, are not in accord to the West Germany efforts to assist Greece financially and promote friendly relationships [...]" (Fleischer, 2009, pp. 530–531).

From the early 60s and especially during the brief "democratic break" from 1963 to 1966, films that projected German crimes with even bigger intensity were created and linked them to the Nazi ideology. This representation was of course in contrast to the Greek government formal politics. The governments kept degrading or silencing German crimes in order to build up friendly relations with the West Germany allies. Most of those films' directors had broader left political beliefs. Furthermore, until 1967, the reference to the Nazi crimes and the Jews' persecutions comprised the main political argument of the communist left.

Within the junta, many films focus on German atrocities disconnecting them from Nazi ideology. Most interesting is that films represent Germans as common criminals, while in two films is underlined the superiority of Greeks against the German Barbarians. This presentation, that would be expected to provoke the reaction of the powerful censorship, is tolerated if not reinforced by the regime of the colonels due to the West Germany attitude, that was applying pressure on this regime and was providing refuge to the junta's opponents, allowing them to continue their action (Psyroukis, 1983, p. 153).

After the reinstatement of democracy and liberation references to the German conquerors are reduced, as the number of films about the occupation was reduced. A regime of freedom that followed the censorship's smothering control lasted from the end of war to the fall of the junta, and therefore, we have films that depict the opinion of the left about the 1940s (Andritsos, 2016, pp. 35–42). In contrast to the films created till 1974 and focused on the occupation, omitting the Civil War, except only the Civil War movies of the dictatorship (Andritsos, 2020, pp. 230–231), there are for the first time films that put occupation aside and focus on the Dekemvriana and the Civil War (Andritsos, 2021).

Although the themes indicated by these films reflect on the general social and political developments, there is not a mechanic and automated correlation between these and the themes raised. The films are not isolated from the social and political contexts, but it would be a mistake if they were mechanically reduced to them. Cinema is not a mirror that shows what happens in society in a passive way (McGee, 1997, p. 21). The first films – *Raid in the Aegean, The Unconquered Slaves, The Last Mission* – functioned as blueprints for the later films and created the main German conquerors' characteristics. Also, in some cases, we notice that the remakes were created many years later, in different social and political contexts (Eagleton, 1981, pp. 80–81). As Pierre Sorlin notes: "Films give birth to films, films mimic films" (1991, p. 10). The similarities between the films *The Island of the Brave, The Dawn of Victory*, and *Isidora* are apocalyptic (Andritsos, 2020, p. 291).

The question of receiving the films' messages by the audience remains open. Although ticket sales are a significant criterion, there is the problem of lack of data about the provinces box offices, as well as the second/follow up screenings of films. We can't really answer the question how the viewers received the aforementioned films. Nor can we watch the films as if we lived in the 1960s; the social, political, and cultural conditions have changed dramatically (McGee, 1997, p. 13). Even people, who watched the films when they were first presented, rewatch them with a different understanding. We may assume that big box office hits had maximum influence compared to less big hits, but we cannot really judge that due to the tickets sold in Athens, disregarding ticket figures in the rest of Greece. The problem of assessing the influence becomes greater, assuming that the working class audience as well as audiences in the provinces attended the second round/follow-up screening choosing films with entirely different criteria (Jenkins, 2000, p. 166).

The critics in the cinema magazines *Kinimatografikos Astir* [The Star of Cinema] and *Theamata* [Spectacles], mainly addressed to the cinema owners, pinpoint how different the audiences are and suggest to them which films to show to satisfy each audience (Saris, 1967, p. 13). Finally, to be able to see the whole picture, we must take into account censorship, the political circumstances especially at times of agitation and the distribution network. Advertising and star system had an important influence on the films' box office as well (Andritsos, 2011, pp. 271–288; Dyer, 2000, pp. 604–605). Moreover, we don't have enough information on how the audiences reacted, if they liked them or if they were disappointed. The films are decoded in a different way by each viewer according to their experiences, political and ideological views. The viewers are not exactly consumers. In many cases, they produce different messages from those the films intend to give (Creed, 1998, p. 205).

Even if we manage to identify the reasons of the films' box office hit, we cannot be certain about how they were received, as we do not have enough evidence on audiences' reactions and overall reception during screenings, and we do not know whether they liked the films or not (Sorlin, 1991, p. 211). Viewing the films does not mean agreeing with their messages. In many cases, viewers criticize what they watch and end up on opinions that are differentiated or even come to contrast with the films creators' intensions (Gripsurd, 1998, p. 205). Films account to several interpretations, and their messages are deciphered differently by each viewer, depending on their experiences and political as well as their ideological preferences.

Nevertheless, we believe that the films that made a big box office hit and/or caused an impact on the public, like: *Bloody Christmas, Barefoot battalion, The Island of the Brave, The Betrayal, The Round Up, With Shine in the Eyes, The Teacher with the Blond Hair, The Mediterranean is Burning, NO, Lieutenant Natasha, What Did You Do in the War, Thanasis?* played the most important part in portraying the German conquerors. Although, the rest of the films contributed to this, on a different degree each one of them, as they added up to the image cinema created about the German conquerors.

REFERENCES

Andritsos, Y. (2011). Occupation and resistance in Greek full length fiction films from 1974 till 1981. In V. Apostolidou & Y. Antoniou (Eds.), *Occupation and civil war in art. New Estia* (Vol. 1.845, pp. 1186–1199).

Andritsos, Y. (2016). Censorship in Greek cinema. In P. Rinelopi & D. Xristopoulos (Eds.), *Censorship in Greece* (pp. 35–42). Rosa Luxembourg Foundation.

Andritsos, Y. (2020). *Cinema and history. Occupation and resistance in Greek full length fiction films from 1945 till 1981*. ΚΨΜ.

Andritsos, Y. (2021). Anti-communism in Greek Cinema. Anti-communist propaganda films from 1967 to 1974. In A. Maratos (Ed.), *Fragments of arts. Fragments of history* (pp. 645–657). Nisos/Nikos Poulantzas Institute.

Art Review. (1958). In the name of the Nation. *Art Review*, 46–48, 4–6.

Creed, B. (1998). Film and psychoanalysis. In H. John & P. C. Gibson (Eds.), *The Oxford guide to film studies* (pp. 77–90). Oxford University Press.

Dudley, A. (1998). Film and history. In H. John & P. C. Gibson (Eds.), *The Oxford guide to film studies* (pp. 176–189). Oxford University Press.

Dyer, R. (2000). Heavenly bodies: Film stars and society. In R. Stam & T. Miller (Eds.), *Film and theory. An anthology*. Blackwell Publishers Ltd.

Eagleton, T. (1981). *Marxism and literary criticism*. Ypsilon.

Eberchard, E. (2007). German antifascists in ELAS. In C. Chatziiosif & P. Papastratis (Eds.), *History of Greece in the twentieth century. World war II-occupation-resistance 1940–1945* (pp. 68–77). Vivliorama.

Elsaesser, T. (1996). Subject positions, speaking positions: From Holocaust, our Hitler and Heimat to Sloah and Schindler's list. In S. Vivian (Ed.), *The persistence of history television and modern event* (pp. 145–183). Routledge.

Fleischer, H. (1995). *Crown and Swastika. Occupation and resistance in Greece 1941–1944*. Papazisis.

Fleischer, H. (2003). Remembrance vs. oblivion. In H. Fleischer (Ed.), *Greece 36–49. From dictatorship to civil war. Sections and continuations* (pp. 11–23). Kastaniotis.

Fleischer, H. (2003–2004). The past beneath the present. The resurgence of world war II after the collapse of communism: A stroll through the international press. *Historein, 4*, 45–130.

Fleischer, H. (2009). *Memory's wars. World war II in public history*. Nefeli.

Grigoriadis, S. History of contemporary Greece 1941–1974. Kapopoulos.

Gripsurd, J. (1998). Film audiences. In H. John & P. Gibson (Eds.), *The Oxford guide to film studies* (pp. 202–211). Oxford University Press.

Heartney, E. (2002). Out of the bunker: A recent exhibition at the Jewish Museum examined the use of Nazi imagery in contemporary art. *Art in America*. www.Findarticles.com

Hobsbawm, E. (1991). *Age of extremes. The short twentieth century, 1914–1991*. Themelio.

Jenkins, H. (2000). Reception theory and audience research: The mystery of the vampire's kiss. In C. Gledhill & L. Williams (Eds.), *Reinventing film studies* (pp. 165–182). Oxford University Press.

Kaes, A. (1990). History and film: Memory in the age of electronic dissemination. *History & Memory, 2*, 110–129.

Linardatos, S. (1977). *From civil war to Junta*. Papazisis.

Mazower, M. (1994). *Inside Hitler's Greece. The experience of occupation 1941–1944*. Alexandria.

McGee, P. (1997). *Cinema, theory and political responsibility*. Cambridge University Press.

Moschovakis, A. (1964, November 24). The Betrayal. *The Dawn*.

Moschovakis, A. (1965, September 28). The Round-Up. *The Dawn*.

Moschovakis, A. (1966, September 27). With Shine in the Eyes. *The Dawn*.

National Archives. (1952, June 24). Archive of the general secretariat of press, confidential documents box 420: Document of the ministry of foreign affairs.

Novick, P. (1999). *The holocaust in American life*. Mariner Books.

Papastratis, P. (1984). *British policy towards Greece during the second world war 1941–1944*. Cambridge University Press.

Pellico. (1947). A sad quarterly. *Cinematographic Star, 586*, 4–6.

Psyroukis, N. (1975). *History of contemporary Greece 1940–1967*. Epikairotita.

Psyroukis, N. (1983). *History of contemporary Greece 1967–1974. The regime of April 21*. Epikairotita.

Rafailidis, V. (1971). Greek full length fiction films. *Modern Cinema, 16*, 11–15.

Saris, N. (1967). Cinematographic motivations in Greece. Why do people go to the cinema? *Spectacle, 223*, 12–15.

Sorlin, P. (1980). *The film in history: Restaging the past*. Barnes and Noble Books.

Sorlin, P. (1991). *European cinemas. European societies 1939–1990*. Rootledge.

Sorlin, P. (1999). Children as war victims in postwar European cinema. In J. Winter & E. Sivan (Eds.), *War and remembrance in the twentieth century* (pp. 104–125). Cambridge University Press.

Stamatiou, K. (1959a, October 27). The Island of the brave. *The Dawn*.

Stamatiou, K. (1959b, October 27). Soldiers without a uniform. *The Dawn*.

The Dawn. (1978a, March 15). Is the government responsible for the bombs?

The Dawn. (1978b, June 21). 15 injured at cinema rex!

The Postman. (1966, March).

Tsirbinos, T. (1971). October 28, 5:30. New State February 2.

Virilio, P. (2005). *Το δικαίωμα στην Αντίσταση* [*The right to resistance*] (P. Kalamaras, Trans.). Article 46.

6

"OTHER" DEBTS: THE GERMAN WWII DEBT TO GREECE IN THE GERMAN PRESS AND "THE GREEK CRISIS" CONTEXT

YIANNIS MYLONAS

HSE University, Russia

Keywords: War reparations; German-Greek relations; media representation; historical accountability; critical discourse analysis

INTRODUCTION: ADDRESSING THE GREEK WAR REPARATION DEMANDS IN THE GERMAN MAINSTREAM PRESS

Now, Germans were people who just came to the island for vacations [...] the island was full of Germans, old, middle aged, people who had been young during the war and now in their prosperity hid their former arrogance behind a fake joviality and the pretence of being merely tourists and nothing else [...] the defeated were the others, the ones who served them during their vacations on a southern island. (De Luca, 2011, pp. 15–16)

The German and Western publics are largely unaware of the atrocities perpetrated in Greece by Nazi Germany (Fleischer, 2003; Radiopoulos, 2019), and of the cycle of violence that followed Greece's liberation, leading to decades of political oppression, autocratic reign, and economic dependency. Even less is publicly known on the ways that the post-war German state has avoided paying war reparations to Greece, while summoning its hegemonic position in Europe and dictating favorable policy regimes to the European periphery. This study aspires in shedding some light to the discursive strategies of Germany's avoidance of debt repayment, and the public articulation of such debt deference strategies in today's German public sphere. Though not involved in the war unleashed by Nazi Germany, the post-war generations of Germany benefited from not paying war reparations to countries Occupied by Nazi Germany. The recognition of such a position can become a source of self-reflection and may generate solidarity politics against the perpetuation of injustice: "socially constituted ignorance and denial are essential components of implication; as such, they are also potential starting points for those who want to transform implication and refigure it as the basis of a differentiated, long-distance solidarity" (Rothberg, 2019, p. 200).

On April 17, 2019, the Greek Parliament voted in favor of pursuing all reparations owed by Germany to Greece for both world wars and World War Two (WWII) in particular, under the initiative of the SYRIZA (Coalition of the Radical Left) party, which led a coalition government at the time. These reparations demands were fully negated by the German government, which stated that "the issue is conclusively settled" (Maltezou & Georgiopoulos, 2019). This article examines the ways that Greece's war reparations are publicly negated, by focusing on 30 relevant articles published in the dailies *FAZ* and *Die Welt*, between 2015 and 2019. In the following sections, the legal, political, and moral foundations of Germany's war reparations obligations are discussed; the details surrounding the Greek demands for war reparations by Germany are explained, demonstrating why and how these reparations, though agreed, were in fact never paid. A qualitative content analysis approach is developed, where the main themes covering the Greek reparations demands found in the specific newspapers, are laid out. The analysis is informed by critical discourse analysis tools (Van Leeuwen, 2008; Wodak, 2015), to explain the argumentative legitimation strategies found in the articles studied.

THE GREEK WAR REPARATION DEMANDS CONTEXTUALIZED

The following two sections will outline the contemporaneity of the Greek demands for war reparations to be paid by Germany. This will be done by revising the discussion of the post-war responsibilities of the German state and German citizens, by referring to political theory on responsibility and guilt for the perpetuation of crimes against humanity, and political economy approaches on systems of dependency and hierarchies of debt. The notion of "the implicated subject" (Rothberg, 2019) will be highlighted, to explain the responsibilities of contemporary Germans for crimes committed in their name. This concept is reflexively connected to post-colonial theory, relating to the direct and indirect forms of benefiting achieved, evident in the continuing inequalities between the center and the periphery, which perpetuate regimes of dependency. The German Occupation of the European periphery during the War reflects colonial relations and practices (Baranovski, 2011; Traverso, 2003), as previously perpetrated by European colonial states (like Germany) across the globe. Additionally, the German war debts will be explained in numerical detail, along with the legal basis of the Greek war demands, while demonstrating Germany's perpetual deference strategies to avoid paying its war debt to Greece, benefiting from West Germany's privileged Cold War position and US support, and Greece's continuous economic dependency from German capital, as well as Greece's post-WWII economic recovery strategy and politics.

ECONOMIC, POLITICAL, AND MORAL REGIMES OF RESPONSIBILITY

Besides the ideological fallacies pursued by Hitler through the means of a total war, Marxist analyses foreground politico-economic reasons to explain WWII and the post-war European politico-economic balance of power. The global economic crisis characterizing the interwar period marked a crucial reason for the Second World War. Accordingly, the fear of communism for Europe's upper classes forms another important reason; the German bourgeois interests aligned with the nationalist, racist and conspirational ideology of nazism to contain communism, and to expand territorially for resources, overcoming the limits of a protectionist global economy, and competing for global hegemony with other imperialist countries (Bambley, 2014). Despite its defeat and partition, (West) Germany's geopolitical position in the Cold War context allowed her to quickly emerge as an important politico-economic actor in the West. This proved to be particularly beneficial to West Germany's reconstruction process, freezing its reparation debt to various countries it formerly occupied, and developing its industrial and export-driven economic basis.

The discussion outlining the dimensions of German responsibility for the Second World War, and the crimes perpetrated in the name of Germany and the German people is a long one, involving political, moral, and economic dimensions. The moral and political dimensions have been prominent in the shaping of post-war German identity and political culture and remain a contested field. The economic dimensions of responsibility, related to both the causes of the war, and Germany's war reparations obligations, have been a matter of juridical debates and procedures, as well as political disputes in formal and informal levels.

The emphasis on the moral and juridical dimensions of responsibility has generally underplayed the politics that organize regimes of responsibility and the economic obligations deriving from it, related to the material definition of Germany's war reparations debt to the countries it caused harm during WWII. Therefore, the economic dimensions of Germany's responsibility as a perpetrator of war and war crimes, are caught in the political and moral discussion of the topic as well, but also downplayed by it. This section will introduce some important arguments regarding the political and moral dimensions of German responsibility, seeing them as intrinsic to the structural and economic understanding of Germany's responsibility for the war and the obligations to the victims, to restore justice.

Karl Jaspers developed four categories of criminal guilt in 1946, to address the legitimacy of the Nuremberg trials to his fellow Germans who disputed it (Rothberg, 2019, p. 42). These categories concern "the criminal guilt of the direct perpetrators, the political guilt of the institutions and organized forces that supported Hitler's power, the individual guilt of the accomplices, and the 'metaphysical' guilt of all citizens who recognized the criminal character of the Nazi regime but accepted it without protesting" (Traverso, 2019, p. 146). Through these categories, Jaspers explains that the responsibility of such crimes is not equally shared by all Germans. While criminal guilt concerns the actual perpetrators of the crimes, the remaining three categories pose a sense of responsibility to all Germans (when considering the categories of political and moral guilt) and possibly to all humans as well (through the notion of metaphysical guilt), for the committed atrocities against humanity. Although criminal and political guilt are connected to the realm of penal law, moral and metaphysical guilt are associated with a reflective and transformative process that may occur on an individual and a collective basis (Rothberg, 2019, p. 44). In Jasper's sense, guilt is meant to develop a sense of historical responsibility for the German nation, in order to assume its position in the international community.

In her "the banality of evil," Hannah Arendt (1992) offered a sharper distinction between guilt and responsibility regarding the degrees of implication in perpetrated crimes, while bringing forth questions of synchronic and diachronic forms of implication (Rothberg, 2019, p. 45). Besides the crime perpetrators' guilt, the synchronic dimension of guilt concerns the bystanders too, bearing moral responsibility for their inactivity. During the Nazi reign, criminality was introduced and legitimized in the public realm and thus all participating in public life became implicated (in different degrees) to the Nazi deeds: "the trouble with Eichmann is that there were so many like him… neither perverted, nor sadistic… and terrifyingly normal" (Arendt, 1992, p. 276). While guilt is synchronous, responsibility has a rather diachronic dimension, "encompassing political communities that are transgenerational… although not guilty of what precedes us, we remain captive to a communal responsibility by virtue of our participation in a collective way of life" (Rothberg, 2019, pp. 46–47). Therefore, guilt is backward looking but responsibility is contemporaneous (Rothberg, 2019, p. 50).

Political responsibility is evoked in both Jasper's and Arendt's work, regarding one's membership in a nation state. The identity of the national citizen should thus be shaped by the responsibility over collective past misdemeanors to advance a democratic ethos in the present and the future. Habermas also engages with political responsibility concerns, while participating in the so-called "historians' debate" in his native Germany during the 1980s. Witnessing the rise of German nationalism, and along with it the gaining ground of historical revisionist arguments that relativized Germany's guilt for the war, Habermas (1989, p. 234) argued for the diachronic dimension of German responsibility. Historical revisionist arguments such as Nolte's "interpretation of the 'European civil war'" put Germany on the side of the victims including the Nazi regime, which was threatened first by a Bolshevik uprising directed from Moscow and then by a war of extermination waged by both Soviet and Allied military forces. The persecutor transformed into a victim: Nolte's revisionism lies in this reversal of the historical perspective" (Traverso, 2019, p. 146). Fleischer (2003. p. 18) pointed that the historians' debate in Germany during the late 20th century split the public into those emphasizing the need to remember to "never experience Nazism again" and those stressing that the discussion of Germany's Nazi past has been enough. For Habermas, there is a need for the public to engage in a constant critical dialogue with the troubling past, to develop a democratic and humanistic culture.

Other scholars (Young, 2011) pursued the broadening of the political sense of responsibility connected to the structural positioning of different national subjects. Here, responsibility is associated with the structural (notably, class) position that subjects occupy, and the organic reproduction of injustices that are naturalized in capitalist societies. In this sense, along with national citizenship, social structure and social class also emerges as key in the allocation of responsibility.

Rothberg (2019, p. 145) addresses the complexity of the matter beyond the perpetrator, victim, and bystander positions. He uses the term "implicated subject" to include subjects that may unconsciously reproduce (and benefit from) injustices. The structural position that subjects occupy is key for the specific conceptualization. The implicated subject does not bear the perpetrator's criminal guilt. Nevertheless, responsibility transcends the actual perpetrators of a crime, and is politically, economically, and morally connected to societal, national, class, or generational affinities. Injustice is understood to emerge from social structures; thus, responsibility can be allocated not only to the guilty perpetrations, but also to the subjects' association with specific social structures (e.g., national and class ones), beyond the individuals' actual control (Young, 2011, p. 45).

The moral, political, economic, and structural dimensions of responsibility are intertwined, understanding the nation-state as a structure in a broader historical geopolitical formation that, along with change, also maintains continuity (Mazower, 2000; Pavone, 2014). According to relevant literature on WWII history (Mazower, 2000, p. 278), the continuation of the state means the persisting of authoritarian elements in Germany (and Italy) after the collapse of fascism and nazism. In this paper, the continuity of state idea is stressed further, to discuss Germany's continuities as a core European state across the 20th century, by understanding the power dynamics involved in the uneven process of establishing and legitimizing demands for war reparations from Germany by a subordinate country; likewise, Greece's continuous peripherality is also stressed. The suppression of the left after Greece's liberation also meant the continuing dependency of Greece to the Western core states, and the toning down of war reparations demands, something that continues in present times as well. The structural dimensions of such unequal power relations are central, connected to political and economic regimes shaping core and peripheral nation states internally and externally. This is further associated with the geopolitical role that Germany played during the Cold War, allowing it to bypass the Greek war reparations demands, as the next section will demonstrate.

THE LEGAL FOUNDATIONS OF THE GREEK REPARATION DEMANDS AND THEIR PERPETUAL AVOIDANCE

Following the defeat of the Italian military expedition to conquer Greece in the late 1940, Nazi Germany declared war to Greece in the spring of 1941, to assist its ally, Fascist Italy. The Germans conquered Greece by the end of May

1941. They proceed then to create three zones of occupation, a German, an Italian, and a Bulgarian one. After Italy's capitulation to the Allies in September 1943, the German zone expanded to the Italian zone too. The Occupation of Greece lasted until October 1944, when the Germans were forced to retreat after the advances of the Red Army in the Balkans, the continuous German losses in all fronts, and the growth of the Greek armed resistance movement across the country.

The Occupation deteriorated Greece economically and socially, leading to the country's prolonged political destabilization, radicalizing pre-existing conflicts and controversies in Greece, and producing new ones as well (Glezos, 2006; Králová, 2013; Liakos, 2003; Margaritis, 2010; Mazower, 2001; Skouras et al., 1991/1947). The German army brought along few provisions, and used all the country's material resources at its disposal. Králová (2013, p. 57) notes that the Germans confiscated everything, from food, to livestock and various materials (e.g., minerals, oil, cotton, tobacco, wood, coil, and machinery), antiquities, and the personal valuables of Greeks, which they sent to Germany. The Germans forced a parallel currency with no actual value, flagging the Greek market.[1] Such practices soon led to the outbreak of a famine that claimed the lives of thousands (estimations range from 40,000 to half a million dead from famine and its long-term effects). Further, the Germans imposed the covering of the Occupation expenses to Greece, which, in line with the destruction of the Greek economy from the above-mentioned pillaging practices, led to high rates of inflation. Most crucially, the German occupying forces perpetrated mass, indiscriminate murders of civilians and the destruction and looting of their belongings, destroying approximately 1,500 villages in retaliation acts (Králová, 2013, p. 73), purged and exterminated the country's Jews at a level of over 65% of their pre-war population and looted their properties, destroyed Greece's public infrastructures

---

[1] The following excerpt may be indicative of the Reichmark's uses and effects in the Greek market: "By using a currency known as 'Occupation Marks' – a currency with no value outside of Greece – German soldiers were ordered to purchase anything and everything from retail outlets and ship the goods home to the Reich, thus devastating the commercial center of Athens [...] From his apartment window in the center of the city, Archer recalls observing a squad of soldiers buying-up a leather-goods shop. They carried their newly acquired suitcases to the clothes shop next door and filled the bags, buying-out this store as well. They then entered the neighboring camera store and emptied that as well. In the space of 30 minutes, three families were put out of business with little chance of restocking and with virtually no money exchanged (Archer, 1944, p. 198). The next stage in the process, Archer testifies, was usually the 'purchase' of the business itself and the installation of a German director. If sale of stock was refused, the owner was arrested and taken into internment. During the first few months of the 1941 occupation an estimated two thousand factories of all sizes had been repossessed in Athens by the German authorities" (Knight, 2015, pp. 67–68).

(like ports, bridges, railways, train cars, roads – even the Corinth canal was blown), and exploited the unpaid labor of thousands of civilians who were violently summarized into forced labor in Greece and in Germany to serve various German needs (Margaritis, 2010, p. 96). Overall, Greece lost 6%–7% of its pre-war population due to the criminal hardships imposed by Nazi Germany (Králová, 2013, pp. 108–109).

Nazi Germany launched a war of annihilation in the East and to a certain degree, in the Balkans as well (Heer et al., 2008; Luther & Stahel, 2020; Stahel, 2015). The deprivation and decimation of native populations (deemed as inferior) was an official policy of Nazi Germany in the East, from Poland to the Soviet Union, to create a "lebensraum" for ethic German settlers and colonizers; the Balkans were also treated with exceptional brutality on equivalent racist principles. The mass antifascist resistance of the people of Greece and Serbia was dealt through terroristic policies of collective responsibility, resulting to the indiscriminate mass execution of civilians and the burning of homes, districts, and, as mentioned above, whole towns and villages. The German occupation conditions in the occupied Soviet Union, Poland, Serbia, and Greece, was way harsher than that in the occupied countries of the Western Europe, the populations of which the Nazis considered as "Aryan" (Handrinos, 2018).

The legendary resistance fighter and life-long leftist activist, Manolis Glezos (2014), argued that the German WWII debt to Greece has three main dimensions: (i) what is owed to the public sector for the total damage that the Occupation caused to the Greek economy, the state infrastructure, etc., (ii) what is owed to the people who suffered by the German atrocities, (iii) what is owed for the forced loan Nazi Germany acquired from the Greek central bank for Occupation expenses. Further demands concern the return of the looted antiquities, as well as compensations for sunken vessels, the expropriation of goods (such as tobacco), or, the expropriation of public and private gold reserves, among other (Poulakidas, 2018).

As was decided by the Paris Allied Treaty in 1946, the amount owed to Greece by Germany for the destruction caused to its national economy, was at $7.1bn (in the 1938 currency value) to be paid by Germany to Greece for war. This was half the sum of Greece's $14.6bn actual demand (Glezos, 2006; Králová, 2013, p. 276). Overall, according to the Greek Interparliamentary Committee working on the German war reparations issue, the total amount of the Greek state demands by Germany for both WWI and WWII is nowadays between 278.736.276.691 and 318.688.098.016 Euros, based on the findings of the Special Committee of the Treasury of the State (Poulakidas, 2018). This sum does not include reparations to war victims (estimated at 22bn) and the forced occupation loan it imposed to Greece (with the sum of 476 million Reichsmarks at 0% interest to Nazi Germany), which in today's currency amounts to $18bn. Up until now, Germany paid only minor sums of its total war-related debts to Greece,[2] avoiding payments through strategies of negotiations delay, politico-economic pressure, and public deception (Králová, 2013; Radiopoulos, 2019, p. 330), utilizing the advantages offered by its geopolitical position in the Cold War especially (Fleischer, 2008).

The Cold War context allowed Germany's rapid rebirth from its utter defeat. Germany was soon to rise into a powerful politico-economic player in the West with the USA's political and economic backing, which made it a front against the Soviet Union and its allies (Anderson, 2009). For this reason, the London Agreement on German External Debts of 1953 decided an indefinite deferring of Germany's WWI and WWII debt to various countries including Greece. According to the London Agreement's rationale, Germany would repay its debts when it begun to have trade surpluses, with repayments limited to 3% of export earnings (Toussaint, 2006). Tsoukalas (1974, p. 102) argued that the allies themselves were unwilling to assist Greece's rather anemic war reparations demands, as they would prefer that Greece remains in dependency, as a peripheral state tied to Western superpowers instead of using the potential resources drawn from the payment of Germany's debt to develop in a more self-sufficient way. The post-war reconstruction of Greece was based upon the funds received by the Marshall plan, and the broader economic planning for the region designed by the US and the advance of the Truman doctrine there. From the early 1950s though, the US was reluctant in continuing funding Greece's restructuring. As Britain also abstained from such a possibility, West Germany emerged as a possible source of investing in Greece, something also conditionally supported by the US (Pelt, 2006). West German capital was also desired by powerful politico-economic agents of Greece (like the leading Greek industrialist, Bodosakis), maintaining a US-oriented vision for Greece's post-war course. For West Germany, investing in Greece's restructuring was an opportunity to resume its pre-war politico-economic position and to establish new markets there (especially after the loss of its previous markets in socialist East Europe). Moreover, as Germany emerged to be vital for Greece's post-war export trade (notably tobacco, large quantities of which were

---

2 For instance, in 1960, Greece received a sum of 115 Marks from West Germany for private compensations to only some categories of Nazi crimes' victims, which amounted to the 3/5 of the total compensations demands for the specific victim categories; other categories of victims (e.g., the civilians murdered or repressed by the German reprisal acts) never received any compensation (Radiopoulos, 2019, p. 325; Králová, 2013, p. 225).

exported to Germany before the war), commercial deals between Greece and West Germany were established shortly after the end of the war, despite US hesitations (Pelt, 2006, p. 107). In this context, the post-war Greek governments, proved unwilling to claim the payment of war reparations by West Germany. After the Greek Civil War, the victorious political right attributed Greece's ruins to the communists, and Greek governments pursued lavish economic deals with Western Germany (Králová, 2013, p. 169). Germany used the Cold-war context to shake off its Nazi stigma, and pressured Greece to provide amnesty to German war criminals. In that sense, the punishment of German war criminals and the reparations' issue itself came to be used and managed opportunistically by both Greece and Germany, with Germany enjoying a superior political and economic position to impose her demands upon Greece.

Greece's economic dependency from Germany undermined the demand for German war reparations. Germany's realpolitik took advantage of Greece's weaknesses, like its administrational shortcomings and its economic needs, to indefinitely postpone and to eventually negate its war reparations obligations (Králová, 2013, p. 363). Likewise, Greece's war reparations' demands were silenced for short-term political and economic gains (Králová, 2013, p. 315). In conclusion, despite the German claims over the closure of the Greek reparation demands, the Greek state never resigned from its war reparations demands (Králová, 2013, p. 331). There was never any agreement for the cancelling, or the expiration of Germany's debt to Greece (Radiopoulos, 2019, p. 326), and Greece never signed the "Treaty on the Final Settlement with Respect to Germany" (known as "2 + 4 agreement") for the unification of Germany (United Nations, 1992).

METHODOLOGY

The analysis is based on the study of 24 articles published in *Die Welt*, and on 6 relevant articles published in FAZ. These articles were accessible at the newspapers' online archival resources and were traced by using the key words "Kriegsentschädigungen," "Kriegsreparationen," "deutsche Kriegsreparationen nach Griechenland," "deutche reparationen," and "griechische Vorwürfe." Established in 1946, *Die Welt* is a popular Germany daily bought by the media conglomerate Axel Springer in 1953. Axel Springer is generally known for its conservative leanings. Founded in 1949, FAZ (Frankfurter

Allgemeine Zeitung) is a liberal-conservative newspaper, owned by the FAZIT Foundation.

The texts studied are both news reports and opinion articles. In principle, newspapers are understood as presenting a specific type of discourse that includes different textual genres and reproduces structures of social power (Van Dijk, 1989, p. 19). Other than offering a view of reality that may be true or false, the news discourse provides us with "a frame through which the social world is routinely constructed" (Van Dijk, 1998, p. 8). While news reports are presented under an objectivist and presumably impartial style, opinion articles are more openly partisan and ideological. Newspaper editors' opinion articles form a particular kind of news media genre, which is crucial in the construction of public opinion, as it delivers input on how to understand news and the various events that are covered by news media. In that sense, editors' opinion-making articles are carries of ideological positions and assumptions, expressing the broader ideological affiliations of the medium. In this study, the opinion articles authored by a chief editor of Die Welt named Sven Felix Kellerhoff are exemplary, as they offer a highly opinionated position disputing the legitimacy of the Greek war reparation demands, attacking the time's left-leaning government of Greece, while also promoting historical revisionist claims that deny the German war reparations obligations.

The method of analysis followed was that of qualitative content analysis (Saldaña, 2011). The texts were read twice and then coded through three main interrelated thematic categories, which emerged after two cycles of coding. These three overarching codes, which entail various related subthemes, are the following: (1) the atrocities perpetrated by Nazi Germany in Greece are not denied, yet this is done tactfully (2) The reparations demands are generally dismissed as false, "old," "legally settled," "populist," and "unrealistic" (3) A focus on "the future" instead of laying war reparations claims is proposed, and expected from Greece. The specific codes are further explained below. The analysis also draws on critical discourse analysis (Van Leeuwen, 2008; Wodak, 2015) to disclose the ways that argumentative legitimacy is accomplished in the newspapers' negating of the Greek reparations demands.

ACKNOWLEDGING ATROCITIES, DENYING REPARATIONS

The crimes committed by the Wehrmacht and the destruction caused by the Germans during the Occupation of Greece are generally acknowledged by all articles. Details over the scale of the atrocities are also occasionally provided:

> *For undoubtedly the Wehrmacht and other German units in the Second World War committed terrible misdeeds almost everywhere in the occupied countries of Europe, which cannot be 'repaired' by anything. How to 'compensate' the murder of up to 80,000 Greek civilians? Or the deportation of almost 59,000 Jews from Greece to German extermination camps? What about the 200,000, perhaps even 500,000, deaths from the famine and civil war that Greece had to undergo during and after the Second World War? (Kellerhoff, 2018)*

The exhibition of war crimes in detail however, in opinion articles such as the above, seems to be deployed to present a moralistic reduction of the war reparations demands. Here, after overemphasizing the German war atrocities perpetrated in Greece, the author comes to conclude the impossibility of ever achieving full compensation. Hence, the reparations' demands appear as unattainable through a dramatic (stressed by rhetorical questions posed) recounting of the Occupation casualties. Such a lyrical acknowledgment of Germany's crimes is in general agreement with the formal position of the German state over its moral liability toward Greece and other countries. Although the crimes are acknowledged, the reparations are negated as supposedly "settled" and closed:

> *The German government, however, once again rejected the demands. 'Germany is absolutely and constantly aware of its historical responsibility for the suffering that National Socialism brought upon many countries in Europe,' said government spokesman Steen Seibert. 'But that does not change our position and our firm conviction that the question of reparations and compensation payments has, in our conviction, been finally and finally settled, concluded'. (Güler et al., 2015)*

Additionally, specific articles point toward further degrees of responsibility, besides the German one, over the crimes committed. Thus, the responsibility of Nazi Germany's allies, Italy and Bulgaria in the Occupation of Greece is also stressed in the discussion of the German Occupation practices. The British naval blockade in Greece is presented as another reason behind the famine caused by the German Occupation. The deeds of the Greek partisans too are mentioned to explain the causes of the German indiscriminate retribution actions. Here, the argumentative topoi of the Nazis are reproduced, who attempted to legitimize their indiscriminate reprisals to the activity of the partisans against the Occupying forces, deploying monstrous stereotypes of the communist villain (Mazower, 2001). To this regard, historical revisionist accounts in Europe, that also appeared in Greece from the 1990s onwards, conceptualized Nazi aggression and crimes as (potentially extreme) responses to communism and the partisans' counter-violence (Kousouris, 2015, p. 241). Violence and counter-violence are thus equated here, in the historical revisionist fashion that whitewashes fascism and nazism. Furthermore, the Greek Civil War, which followed shortly after Greece's liberation, is presented as something that supposedly brought worse misfortunes to Greece than the Occupation itself, relativizing the Occupation, and underplaying the historical connections of the Occupation and Greece's Civil War (Voglis, 2014, p. 49).

> *Greek politicians are often heard to say that Greece is one of the states that suffered most under the German occupation in the Second World War. That is true, but incomplete; for there were three states that occupied Greece. The correct term should be German-Italian-Bulgarian occupation - at least until the end of 1943, when Italy withdrew. Accordingly, Prime Minister Alexis Tsipras would have to address reparation demands not only to Berlin, but also to Rome and Sofia. Although this does not change anything about the crimes committed by the Germans, it could even be argued, with a little exaggeration, that the Greeks had Italy to thank for Hitler's armies invading Greece in April 1941[...] The British naval blockade further exacerbated the famine [...] Not all the destruction, however, was perpetrated by Germans. A small British squad parachuted in was very successful with acts of sabotage. It particularly targeted the Thessaloniki-Athens railway line, which was crucial for supplying the Afrika Korps. At the end of 1942, the British and local partisans succeeded in one of the most spectacular acts of sabotage of the war by blowing up the bridge over the Gorgopotamos Gorge, which is still impressive today. As a deterrent, the Wehrmacht took to allowing respected Greeks to travel on trains as hostages in freight cars secured with barbed wire [...] The British naval blockade and German looting also exacerbated the famine in Greece. When the first winter of occupation ended in 1942, more than 100,000 Greeks had starved to death. Under American pressure, the British had to ease their blockade so that the Swiss Red Cross could bring food to Greece. Thus, the number of deaths from starvation fell. When the Wehrmacht withdrew in October 1944, it left the war there. The Greek civil war, which continued to bring death and destruction, did not end until 1949. (Martens, 2015)*

Although such references are not nominally denying German responsibility, they are nevertheless lessening and relativizing it, while distributing it to other agents as well. The Nazi German propaganda too, was in fact attributing the famine to the British blockade and to "Jewish profiteers," and the Wehrmacht retributions were being attributed to the partisan activities. Additionally, the Greek Civil War is presented as disconnected from the German Occupation and the divisions it augmented in the Greek society, the arming of the Greek reaction to fight the Resistance, along with the class injustices that the Occupation deepened.

DISMISSING REPARATIONS: OLD, SETTLED, POPULIST

Nearly all articles state that the issue of the German war reparation payments to Greece is "settled and closed." Some ambivalence is expressed in few articles for the occupation loan repayment (Ismar, 2015). The Greek war reparation demands from Germany are generally dismissed as "old," as "legally settled," as "vague" and "populist," and as "unrealistic" and potentially harmful for the Greek economy and for Greece's European trajectory.

The main argumentative topoi (Wodak, 2015, p. 53) evoked to deny the legitimacy of the Greek war reparation demands are those of scientific and legalistic authority. Specific experts are presented stating that such demands have either been settled, paid, or are unclear and politically "biased." Such experts' voices are generally amplified by the articles studied, along with references to specific post-war agreements (notably the "2 + 4 treaty"), to international law articles and to legal outcomes on relevant court cases, to dispute the legality of the reparations demands.

> *Athens wants 278.7 billion euros from Germany; the concrete number is indifferent; the claims can be at 100 billion euros or 500 or 800 billion: It is about building political-moral pressure. For the question of reparations is regulated conclusively under international law: first, by the global agreement between the governments in Athens and Bonn of March 1960; second, by Greece's implicit approval of the two-plus-four treaty of 1990. There is no doubt about that. In the 1953 London Debt Agreement, the regulation of Germany's reparations was postponed to a future peace treaty. This arrangement was made obsolete by the two-plus-four treaty of 1990. Greece cannot sue*

> *Germany; it is unlikely that international courts will override this clear legal position. (Kellerhoff, 2018)*

As this excerpt shows, the reparations' demands appear in ambiguous terms. The sum is not clarified and is presented as arbitrarily defined. This manifestation of vagueness reduces the reparations demands to a matter of "political and moral pressure" associated with the time's political affairs such as the Greek debt crisis. A process of semantic disembedding thus occurs (Fairclough, 2003, p. 68), where the meaning of the war reparation demands is decontextualized from its historical context and placed in a semantic framework negating war reparations' payment. The negation of the war reparations demands is followed by disclaimers such as the following "there is no doubt about that," "it is unlikely that courts will override this clear legal position," meant to create a sense of certainty over the presumed irrelevance of these demands, through the evocation of legal authority.

> *For decades, Greek politicians have been expressing the demands that their country has over Germany [...] Now, however, research suggests that Germany may not be indebted to Greece, but the reverse case may actually be the case: The Greek government may actually be indebted to tens of millions of euros to Berlin, depending on whether one calculates the interest and compound interest rates, in addition to the many billions Greece has received in the context of the various rescue packages for the sake of the euro rescue. This is the result of a thorough investigation of German files, above all a report of the Reichsbank received by the historian Heinz A. Richter.*
> *(Kellerhoff, 2016)*

The categories of intertextuality and interdiscursivity are central in understanding the position of the studied texts within a broader discursive and ideological framework (Fairclough, 2003, p. 47). Richter is often cited by Kellerhoff to provide epistemic legitimacy to claims against the war reparation demands. Drawing on Richter, Kellerhoff not only denies the actuality of the Greek demands (iterating Richter's assertion that reparations were already paid) but even overturns the argument, suggesting that Greece in fact owes Germany war-related loans.

For Margaritis (2015), Richter is developing "a historical revisionist argument towards the rehabilitation of Nazism and its military practices." Richter attempts to equalize the destruction that the Nazis caused in Greece to the deeds of the Greek Resistance to defend and to liberate the country from the Nazi-German aggression. Richter's arguments thus resemble those of Ernst

Nolte, reducing Nazism to a mere reaction to the Russian Revolution and the Bolsheviks' rise to power (Traverso, 2007, p. 140). In a joint article, the historians Fleischer et al. (2016) criticized Richter's controversial work, exposing methodological problems, related to his insufficient archival and sources usage, and his inadequate familiarization with relevant bibliography, deployed to develop a revisionist ideological argument on Germany's historical responsibilities. According to these authors, Richter copies and makes use of the arguments developed by the Nazis and Nazi collaborators, to formulate his claims and allegations. Kellerhoff confronted these scholars, in defense of Richter, in the following way:

> *Of course, the historian Fleischer, the doctor Roth and the lawyer Schminck-Gustavus in their progressivist one-sidedness claim that reparations still have to be paid. This is wrong, but it falls under the freedom of expression. Their reliance on partisan publications is their right – the fact that they present such books as 'standard works', violates the good scientific practice [...] The background of this aggression is apparently a decades sustained resentment of Hagen Fleischer to [Richter], who, in contrast to him has received a professorship at a German university [...] If you consider evaluating the next co-author by scientific standards, you will find interesting information. The physician and former SDS [Socialist German Student League] activist, Karl Heinz Roth, was arrested in 1975 along with a radical-left bank robber, Werner Sauber, member of the June 2 movement who murdered a police officer [...].*
> (Kellerhoff, 2016b)

The discrediting of Fleischer, Roth, and Schminck-Gustavus primarily occurs through references to scientific authority (Van Leeuwen, 2008, p. 109). Scientific authority is both personal (by positioning Richter as an indisputable expert, supposedly overshadowing the professionalism of his critics, who are presented through an emphasis of a differential vocational background, "the doctor Roth and the lawyer Schminck-Gustavus"), and impersonal (through references to nominal entities such as "standard works," "a professorship at a German university," "scientific standards"). Laid by the meagre knowledge status of a certain newspaper editor, these features emerge as irrefutable standards of scientific judgment that no-one can question. The politicization of the work of these authors as broadly "progressive" is further meant to delegitimize it as "one-sided" and biased, and a mere exercise of their liberal right to the "freedom of expression." Nominalizations ("progressives," "partisan publications") and conceptual metaphors ("WWII Tsipras' style" [referring to the time's leftist Greek Prime Minister]) construct in reductionist terms the work and authority of the specific critical authors (Fairclough, 2003, p. 145). The use of a psychological type of motive (Fleischer's alleged spite against Richter) also serves the discrediting of these authors' scientific authority, through a sensualistic argument. This way, we can see the mitigating strategies developed by Kellerhoff to represent the ingroup and outgroup relations in the specific dispute, related to those in defense of the Greek demands for war reparations, and those against them (Reisigl & Wodak, 2001, p. 45).

Proposing Futures: "Realism" Instead of "Populism"

> *Anyway, in Greece substantial parts of the [war reparations] money would percolate into corruption, as happened with the individual compensation payments paid between 1950 and 1960. (Kellerhoff, 2016b)*

Nominalisations with negative connotations, such as "populism" and "corruption" are deployed to discredit Greece, by utilizing familiar culturalist tropes of the Greek crisis. Greece is thus represented as inherently corrupt and its politics as "populist," a term that is meant to discredit non-liberal politics as irrational, non-realistic, and unreliable. A "common-sense" claim over the corrupt nature of "the Greeks" is iterated here in an essentialist and a-historical way. Corruption is reproduced as a perennial trait of "the Greeks," interdiscursively connected to the mainstream "Greek crisis" narrative reproduced by the German government and the German media. This renders the reparations demands illegitimate but also futile, as, even if the reparations are to be paid, they will only end up being devoured by Greece's corruption. Therefore, a racist argumentative topos emerges, interdiscursively linked with the "Greek crisis" cultural-racist stereotypes advanced in Germany (Ervedosa, 2017).

The dismissal of the Greek war reparations demands as "unrealistic," "populist," and even "stupid" (Gabriel nennt griechische Forderung dumm, 2015) is followed by proposals on what should be done instead. Following Joachim Wilhelm Gauck (the times' German President), a "German fund for the future" should be founded, which may finance educational and scientific activities connected to the period of the German Occupation of Greece. The fund should form the basis of a mutual compromise between the two countries over issues related to the German war crimes in Greece. Some newspaper articles are supportive of this idea, while reservation on the fund is also expressed: "Who would want to believe that in connection with the Greek billions in claims, the German side is seriously coming up with something that is supposed to get by with just one million euros a year, on a program that is limited to four years?" (Vitzthum, 2015).

The prevailing proposal offered to resolve the reparations' dispute, is a "realist" one, according to which, Greece should drop the false or "populist" demands for war reparations and should instead work to overcome its debt crisis in friendly terms with Germany and its European partners. War reparations demands create problems and misunderstandings in foreign policy; most importantly, they may provoke other countries (like Poland) to seek reparations demands from Germany in the future, something that may threaten the established EU cohesion and Germany's hegemonic position there. On a social level too, they may jeopardize Greece's economy by disappointing German tourists who may not choose Greece for their vacations. Likewise, "the past" should be put aside; a future-orientated approach should guide Greece and Germany to avoid war in the future:

> *The only way to deal with these burdens of the past is to work it up and make constant efforts to make similar confrontations in the present and future unlikely. This is where populist reparations demands are counterproductive. (Kellerhoff, 2019)*

"Populism" is associated with the politics and the identity of the leftist government of Greece at that time. The liberal European establishment dismiss populism as something opportunist, not serious and unrealistic, despite that democracy is by default populist (Mouffe, 2018). The "counterproductive" nature of such demands is explained through realistic arguments, grounded on economistic and expert-orientated political principles. The Greek politics should be realistic to advance Greece's European potential, while avoiding the risk of politico-economic retributions. An authoritarian argumentative topos (Van Leeuwen, 2008, p. 108) is evident here, coming from the rather impersonal evaluation of reparations' dispute and the conformity suggested to Greece. A moralistic and apolitical assessment of the war reparations as a "burden" of the past, related with (past) "confrontations," reduces the reparations demands into an abstraction that should be somehow resolved for a presumably better "present" and "future" to emerge. Passive voice ("worked up") and nominalizations ("counter-productive") prevailing in the above utterance, lack of concreteness toward the problem and its solution, eradicating agency, and implying mutuality in a highly uneven politico-economic and historical dispute. The politically and economically mightiest EU country, Germany, emerges as the one with the moral and intellectual authority to determine the scope of the Greek-German relations, dictating to the weaker part (Greece) the confines of its political aspirations and conduct, and even the limits of the sayable. This comes to the serving of the politico-economic interests of Germany at the expense of those of Greece, while highlighting Germany's favorable historical sensibilities and uses of memory.

CONCLUSION – HIERARCHIES OF DEBT

Then, as you recall, you told me that the war is over. But the war is not over, because no war is ever over. ("The War, 1945," Anagnostakis, 2000)

The analysis showed that the Greek reparations demands are negated through seemingly a-political arguments that stress expert-driven authority and political realism against "populism," displacing the discussion of Germany's WWII responsibility through ahistorical references that highlight the focus on a present and a future oblivious to the past. Historical revisionism is introduced in varying degrees; while the German atrocities are not nominally negated, responsibility is relativized, and the politico-economic obligations deriving from this responsibility are dismissed.

The European historical revisionist tradition is highly conservative, often aiming at rehabilitating fascism and promoting anti-communism, obfuscating the historical and structural context as well as the value system of communism, falsely equated to what is in fact its rival ideology, fascism (Traverso, 2019). To this regard, the dimension of class is also central in such a discussion. Class is often absent in the historical revisionist arguments, where the structural dimensions of revolution are dismissed and crude realpolitik positions, or narrow cost–benefit analysis approaches are advanced instead to conceptualize resistance and collaborationism (Kostopoulos, 2016; Voglis, 2014, p. 25). Class is also underplayed in national resistance narratives, conceptualizing the Resistance against the nazi-fascist occupation in terms of national liberation, even though, the revolutionary and class politics and class structure dimensions were also central to the formation of majoritarian left-wing resistance movements across Occupied Europe. The mass resistance in Greece had a peasant and worker basis, further attracting middle class segments like students and intellectuals. The lower classes suffered disproportionately from the Occupation; the victims of famine, reprisals, slave labor, and property looting by the nazis and their collaborators were predominately poor peasants, workers, veterans of the war in Albania (against fascist Italy), or impoverished minor Asia refugees. The Greek bourgeoisie collaborated or was able to survive based on its property, while also aspiring poor met rapid social elevation through collaborationist practices (Haralambidis, 2012; Mazower, 2001). Likewise, the Greek bourgeoisie braced the repression of the leftist Greek resistance movement, by supporting right-wing anticommunist paramilitary groups, and the British and later US military and political involvement in the post-war Greek affairs.

While considering the war reparations debt of Germany owed to Greece, and the contemporary Greek sovereign debt, owed mainly to Germany for the recapitalization of the (private) German banking system exposed to the Greek state debt, one may notice two different attitudes on debt repayment. Greece is expected to pay its debt in full; the essence of the Greek sovereign debt is neither questioned, nor it's socio-economic, humanitarian, and political effects, are being accounted for by the mainstream media in Germany and elsewhere. The German war reparations debt to Greece though is generally dismissed, with the Greek bourgeois politicians also abstaining from pursuing the payment of Germany's debt, while also arguing for an oblivion supposedly committed to "the future" (Skertsos: the discussion for the German war reparations belongs to the past, 2023). These seemingly double standards on debt repayment mark the limit of bourgeois ideology and politics. For Althusser (2014, p. 125), the bourgeois is not to succumb to any sort of economic demands, and cannot risk any political compromise on related issues, as its status quo may be jeopardized. Roos (2019, p. 29) showed that the structural power of finance blocks any possibilities of default or debt challenging, to preserve the neoliberal global economic system and the interests it supports.

Contemporary debt politics are meant to sustain the North/Western hegemony, the continuous exploitation of the politico-economically subordinate periphery, as well as to conceal the historical legacies of imperialism, colonialism and fascism and to avoid paying the debts owed to colonized people. In this context, the Greek sovereign debt is much more central for the capitalist system's viability, than the German WWII debt owed to Greece (and to other countries too). The bourgeois establishment is indifferent to such historical sensibilities and claims for justice, restoration, and recognition.

REFERENCES

Althusser, L. (2014). *On the reproduction of capitalism: Ideology and ideological state apparatuses.* Verso.

Anagnostakis, M. (2000). *Τα Ποιήματα 1941–1971* [*The poems 1941–1971*]. Nefeli.

Anderson, P. (2009). *The new old world.* Verso.

Arendt, H. (1992). *The banality of evil, Eichmann in Jerusalem.* Penguin.

Bambley, C. (2014). *The second world war: A Marxist history.* Pluto Press.

Baranovski, S. (2011). *Nazi empire: German colonialism and imperialism from Bismarck to Hitler.* Cambridge University Press.

De Luca, E. (2011). *Me, you* (B.A. Brombert, Trans.). Other Press. (Original work published 1998).

Ervedosa, C. (2017). The calibanisation of the south in the German public "euro crisis" discourse. *Postcolonial Studies, 20*(2), 137–162.

Fairclough, N. (2003). *Analyzing discourse: Textual analysis for social research.* Routledge.

Fleischer, H. (2003). Memories and the oblivious. In H. Fleischer (Ed.), *Greece '36–49: From dictatorship to civil war, ruptures and continuities* (pp. 11–24). Kastaniotis.

Fleischer, H. (2008). *Πόλεμοι μνήμης: Ο Δεύτερος Παγκόσμιος Πόλεμος στη σύγχρονη δημόσια ιστορία* [*Memory wars: The second world war in contemporary public history*]. Nefeli.

Fleischer, H., Roth, K.-H., & Schminck-Gustavus, C. (2016). Die Opfer und nicht die Täter sollen in der Bringschuld sein? Zur Medienkampagne gegen die griechischen Reparationsansprüche aus dem Zweiten Weltkrieg [The victims and not the perpetrators should be in the debt? On the media campaign against Greek reparations claims from the second world war]. *Zeitschrift für Geschichtswissenschaft, 64*(4), 379–388.

Gabriel nennt griechische Forderung dumm [Gabriel calls Greek demand stupid]. (2015, April 07). *Faz.* https://www.faz.net/aktuell/politik/ausland/athen-deutsche-reparationsschuld-liegt-bei-278-7-milliarden-euro-13524838.html

Glezos, M. (2006). *Η Μαύρη Βίβλος της Κατοχής* [*The Black Bible of the occupation*]. Nationalrat für die Entschädigungsforderungen Griechenlands an Deutschland.

Glezos, M. (2014, August 22). Τα τρία είδη οφειλών της Γερμανίας στην Ελλάδα [The three kinds of German debt to Greece]. *Eleytherotypia*. http://www.enet.gr/?i=news.el.article&id=440143

Güler, C., Martens, M., Piller, T., & Tillmann, U. (2015, March 11). Der Streit um das Distomo-Massaker [The dispute over the Distomo massacre]. *FAZ*. https://www.faz.net/aktuell/wirtschaft/konjunktur/griechenland/gerichtsprozesse-um-das-massaker-von-distomo-13476816.html. Accessed on December 28, 2021.

Habermas, J. (1989). *The new conservatism: Cultural criticism and the historians' debate*. MIT Press.

Handrinos, I. (2018). *Πόλεις σε Πόλεμο* [*Cities at war*]. Mov Skiouros.

Haralambidis, M. (2012). *Η Εμπειρία της Κατοχής και της Αντίστασης στην Αθήνα* [*The experience of the occupation and the resistance in Athens*]. Alexandreia.

Heer, H., Manoschek, W., Pollak, A., & Wodak, R. (Eds.). (2008). *The discursive construction of history*. Palgrave Macmillan.

Ismar, G. (2015, March 16). Ein fonds koennte streit um reparationen schlichten [A fund could settle disputes over reparations]. *Die Welt*. https://www.welt.de/geschichte/article138454519/Ein-Fonds-koennte-Streit-um-Reparationen-schlichten.html

Kellerhoff, S. F. (2016, February 15). Hat Griechenland noch Schulden bei Deutschland? [Is Greece still in debt to Germany?]. *Die Welt*. https://www.welt.de/geschichte/zweiter-weltkrieg/article152255024/Hat-Griechenland-noch-Schulden-bei-Deutschland.html?wtrid=onsite.onsitesearch

Kellerhoff, S. F. (2016b, May 9). So wird ein deutscher Griechenlandkenner niedergemacht [A German Greek expert is cut down]. *Die Welt*. https://www.welt.de/geschichte/zweiter-weltkrieg/article155181285/So-wird-ein-deutscher-Griechenlandkenner-niedergemacht.html

Kellerhoff, S. F. (2018, October 08). Reparationen von Deutschland neuer maertyrerort Griechenland fordert 280 milliarden Euro [New place of martyrdom – Greece calls for 280 billion euros]. *Die Welt*. https://www.welt.de/geschichte/article181802900/Reparationen-von-Deutschland-Neuer-Maertyrerort-Griechenland-fordert-280-Milliarden-Euro.html

Kellerhoff, S. F. (2019, May 21). Zweiter Weltkrieg Reparationen heilen nichts [Reparation payments do not heal – They create new problems]. *Die Welt*. https://www.welt.de/debatte/kommentare/plus193790071/Zweiter-Weltkrieg-Reparationen-heilen-nichts.html

Knight, D. (2015). *History, time, and economic crisis in central Greece*. Palgrave MacMillan.

Kostopoulos, T. (2016). Κόκκινος Δεκέμβρης: Το ζήτημα της επαναστατικής βίας [*Red December: The question of revolutionary violence*]. Vivliorama.

Kousouris, D. (2015). Δωσιολογισμός και ιστοριογραφία: Από την πολιτική, στην κοινωνική ιστορία του δωσικογισμού [Collaborationism and historiography: From the political to the social history of collaborationism]. In K. Gardika, A. M. Droumpouki, V. Karamanolakis, & K. Raptis (Eds.), *Η μακριά σκιά της δεκαετίας του 1940: Πόλεμος, Κατοχή, Αντίσταση, Εμφύλιος* [*The long shadow of the 1940's: War, occupation, resistance, civil war*] (pp. 229–244). Alexandria.

Králová, K. (2013). *Στη σκιά της Κατοχής: Οι Ελληνογερμανικές σχέσεις την περίοδο 1940–2010* [*In the shadow of the occupation: The Greek-German relations during the period of 1940–2010*]. Alexandreia.

Liakos, A. (2003). Αντάρτες και συμμορίτες στα αμφιθέατρα [Partisans and bandits in university amphitheaters]. In H. Fleischer (Ed.), *Greece '36–49: From dictatorship to civil war, ruptures and continuities* (pp. 25–36). Kastaniotis.

Luther, G. W. H., & Stahel, D. (2020). *Soldiers of Barbarossa: Combat, genocide, and everyday experiences on the Eastern front, June–December 1941*. Stackpole Books.

Maltezou, R., & Georgiopoulos, G. (2019, April 17). Greek parliament calls on Germany to pay WW2 Reparations. *Reuters*. https://www.reuters.com/article/us-greece-germany-reparations/greek-parliament-calls-on-germany-to-pay-ww2-reparations-idUSKCN1RT1PL

Margaritis, G. (2010). Η κρίση της αποθησαύρισης, η μετατροπή εισοδημάτων σε περιουσιακά στοιχεία στα χρόνια της Κατοχής (1941–1944) [The crisis of accumulation, the transformation of profits into assets during the Occupation (1941–1944)]. In V. Kardasis & A. Psaromilingkos (Eds.), *Μια προδομένη υπόθεση, Γερμανικές αποζημιώσεις, το κόστος της Κατοχής σε αίμα και χρήμα, Ιστορικά Ελευθεροτυπίας* [*A betrayed case, German reparations, the cost of the occupation in blood and in money, Istorika Eleytherotypias*] (pp. 93–106). Tegopoulos.

Margaritis, G. (2015, December 8). Και πάλι (δυστυχώς) για τον κ. Ρίχτερ... [On Mr. Richter again (unfortunately)...]. *Imerodromos*. https://www.imerodromos.gr/margaritis-richter/

Martens, M. (2015, March 12). Wer Deutschland sagt, muss auch Italien sagen [Whoever says Germany must also say Italy]. *FAZ*. https://www.faz.net/aktuell/politik/europaeische-union/griechenland-die-kriegsverbrechen-deutschlands-italiens-und-bulgariens-13477565.html

Mazower, M. (2000). Changing trends in the historiography of postwar Europe, east and west. *International Labor and Working-Class History, 52*, 275–282.

Mazower, M. (2001). *Inside Hitler's Greece: The experience of occupation, 1941–44*. Yale University Press.

Mouffe, C. (2018). *For a left populism*. Verso.

Pavone, C. (2014). *A civil war: A history of the Italian resistance*. Verso.

Pelt, M. (2006). *Tying Greece to the west: US-West German-Greek relations, 1949–1974*. Museum Tusculanum Press.

Poulakidas, K. (2018, February 14). Έως και 426 δισ. ευρώ οφείλει η Γερμανία [Germany owes up to 426bn]. *Avgi*. http://www.avgi.gr/article/10811/9248601/eos-kai-426-dis-euro-opheilei-e-germania

Radiopoulos, A. (2019). *Η διεκδίκηση των γερμανικών οφειλών προς την Ελλάδα, από τον Α' και τον Β' Παγκόσμιο Πόλεμο μέσα από έγγραφα του αρχείου του Υπουργείου Εξωτερικών* [*The demands for the German debt to Greece from the first and the second world war through the documents of the foreign ministry account*]. Nefeli.

Reisigl, M., & Ruth Wodak, R. (2001). *Discourse and discrimination: Rhetorics of racism and antisemitism*. Routledge.

Roos, J. (2019). *Why not default? The political economy of sovereign debt.* Princeton University Press.

Rothberg, M. (2019). *The implicated subject: Beyond victims and perpetrators.* Stanford University Press.

Saldaña, J. (2011). *The coding manual for qualitative researchers.* Sage.

Skertsos: The discussion for the German war reparations belongs ot the past. (2023, May 12). *The Press Project.* https://thepressproject.gr/skertsos-i-syzitisi-gia-tis-germanikes-apozimioseis-anikei-sto-parelthon-gia-aparadektes-kai-anistorites-diloseis-kanei-logo-o-syriza/

Skouras, F., Hatzidimos, A., Kaloutsis, A., & Papadimitriou, G. (1991/1947). *Η ψυχοπαθολογία της πείνας, του φόβου και του άγχους* [*The psychopathology of hunger, fear and anxiety; neuroses and psychoneuroses, from the medical chronicle of the occupation*]. Odysseus.

Stahel, D. (2015). *The battle for Moscow.* Cambridge University Press.

Toussaint, E. (2006, October 24). The Marshall plan and the debt agreement on German debt. http://www.cadtm.org/The-Marshall-Plan-and-the-Debt

Traverso, E. (2003). *The origins of nazi violence.* New Press.

Traverso, E. (2007). The new anti-communism. In M. Haynes & J. Wolfreys (Eds.), *History and revolution, refuting revisionism* (pp. 138–155). Verso.

Traverso, E. (2019). *The new faces of fascism, populism and the far right.* Verso.

Tsoukalas, K. (1974). *Η Ελληνική τραγωδία: Από την Απελευθέρωση ως τους Συνταγματάρχες* [*The Greek tragedy: From liberation to the colonels*]. Olkos.

United Nations. (1992). *Treaty on the final settlement with respect to Germany.* https://treaties.un.org/doc/Publication/UNTS/Volume%201696/volume-1696-I-29226-English.pdf

Van Dijk, T. (1989). Structures of discourse and structures of power. *Communication Yearbook, 12,* 18–59.

Van Dijk, T. (1998). *News as discourse.* Lawrence Erlbaum Associates, Publishers.

Van Leeuwen, T. (2008). *Discourse and practice: New tools for critical analysis.* Oxford University Press.

Vitzthum, T. S. (2015, April 12). Deutschlands wackliges alibi im reparationen-streit [War billions: Germany's shaky alibi in the reparations' dispute]. *Die Welt.* https://www.welt.de/politik/deutschland/article139418563/Deutschlands-wackliges-Alibi-im-Reparationen-Streit.html

Voglis, P. (2014). *Η αδύνατη επανάσταση. Η κοινωνική δυναμική του Εμφυλίου Πολέμου* [*The impossible revolution. The social dynamics of the civil war*]. Alexandreia.

Wodak, R. (2015). *The politics of fear: What right-wing populist discourses mean.* Sage.

Young, I. M. (2011). *Responsibility for justice.* Oxford University Press.

7

MISREPRESENTATION OR JUSTIFICATION? THE POLITICS OF GREEK CIVIL WAR MEMORY THROUGH THE CASE OF A PALIMPSEST MEMORIAL

THEODOROS KOUROS

Cyprus University of Technology, Cyprus

Keywords: Memorials; collective memory; Greek civil war; monumental art; historical revisionism

INTRODUCTION

In the United States, one of the most iconic monuments to the Civil War is called "Moment of Mercy." It depicts a soldier offering water to a wounded soldier of the opposing camp. On the contrary, the rationale of the Greek monuments and memorials to the Greek Civil War (GCW) was initially one-sided, partaking on the side of the victors, that is, the National Army. This was part of the wider Greek state strategy at the time most of these memorials were erected. In the first three decades following the end of the GCW, there was an attempt to consolidate the military victory of the National Army at the expense of the Democratic Army of Greece (DSE), in the sphere of ideas, by utilizing various Ideological State Apparatuses (Althusser, 2010). The institutions through which this was attempted included education, the military, the church, and many others. In this chapter, I argue that yet another way in which this consolidation was attempted was monumental and memorial art, that is, monuments and memorials that were erected after the end of the civil war and have direct or indirect references to it. I shall also examine the transformations of collective memory and the impact of such transformations on monuments and memorials, through the case of a palimpsest memorial in Kefalovriso, a village located in close proximity to the Greek-Albanian border (see map), where the last acts of the GCW unfolded. In the Merriam-Webster dictionary, a palimpsest is (1) writing material (such as a parchment or tablet) used one or more times after earlier writing has been erased, (2) something having usually diverse layers or aspects apparent beneath the surface. As I will illustrate in this chapter, this particular memorial is one where names have been added and erased, according to the dominant narrative pertaining to social memory in different points in time.

As Koliopoulos and Veremis note, (2009, pp. 124–125), in July and August of 1949, the final year of the GCW, "the National Army cleared the mountain strongholds near the northern frontiers where the bulk of the DSE was now concentrated. Its culminating victories were the successive capture of Vitsi and then Grammos, where DSE forces totaling 12,000 [...] After losing 3,000 killed or captured, the Democratic Army retreated in good order across the frontier on August 30." Even though this was not the end of guerrilla activity in the area, it was the beginning of the end. Soon after that, the GCW ended, leaving ruins and trauma behind, especially in the wider area under study. The memorial in Kefalovriso offers itself as a representative case, where social memory is manipulated and altered with additions and alterations of who is to be a hero (and, by consequence, who is not), depending on antagonisms and contestations between actors within society, representations of the past as well as aspirations for the present and future (see Mitchell, 2003; Papadakis, 2003). This chapter is based on an article published in a different form, in Greek in Ethnologia online (Kouros, 2016).

MEMORIALS, MONUMENTS, AND STATE POWER

The relationship between memory and history is a long-debated one. Yet the question whether history can be reduced to memory, as some postmodern thinkers have suggested, calls for unpacking. Paul Ricoeur points out the important contribution that the process of forgetting has into history. Memory is highly selective, and collective, it has historical roots, and is realized "in public anniversaries, rituals, and celebrations" (2006, p. 11), which remember and *amplify* specific aspects of the past, and *forget others* that do not fit into its ideology, thus contributing to of collective identity construction and

Misrepresentation or Justification? 109

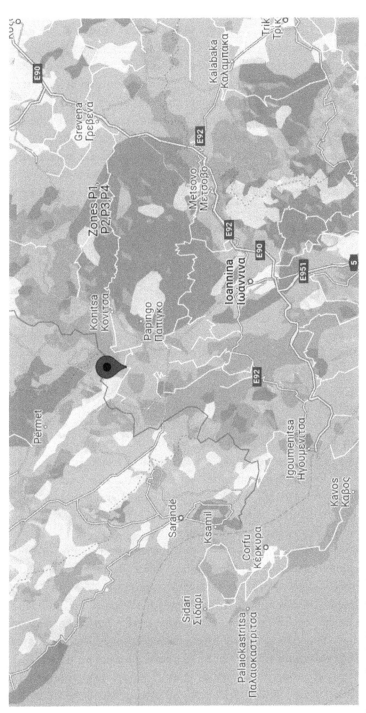

Source: Google Maps. (2023). *Map of Kefalovriso, Greece*. Available at: https://www.google.com/maps/place/Kefalovryso+440+06,+Greece/40.0161684,20.5585317,17.78z/data=!4m6!3m5!1s0x135bb29da8ead6e7:0x500bd2ce2b9d3d0!8m2!3d40.0139525!4d20.5590173!16zL20vMDRfeWxt?entry=ttu [Accessed April 2023].

Map: Kefalovriso's Location.

perpetuation. Ricoeur notes that narratives of memory circulate in conversations and everyday discourse. "By contrast, historical narratives, in their critical function of establishing facts and seeking explanations, break with the discourse of memory" (Iggers, 2009, p. 124). Most postmodernists doubt that an accurate telling of the past is possible and blur the distinction between fact and fiction. Some even go as far to claim that all historical accounts are nothing more than fiction. For Foucault, truth and knowledge are merely constructs to persuade others. They do not need to match reality, as we construct our own reality in such a way as to give us power over others (Poster, 1984). According to Poole (2008, p. 157), "collective memory is presented, not as an attempt to represent the past; but as the process in which a certain past is constructed," creating therefore a "strong temptation to ignore the reference to an actual past." Bal notes that "cultural memorization" may be seen "as an activity occurring in the present, in which the past is continuously modified and redescribed even as it continues to shape the future" (Bal et al., 1999, p. vii).

As Antoniou (2007) notes, the Greek word for "truth," a-lethe-ia, suggests an absence of forgetfulness, making oblivion the antithesis of truth (the alter ego of Memory is the goddess Lethe which is translated as oblivion or forgetfulness). Pierre Nora hinted at a division between the "community of knowledge" and the "community of memory," with historians often neglecting the complex interplay of personal experiences, memories, and historiographical knowledge. Critical theory has explored historiography's role as a nationalist enterprise within nation-states. This complex relationship raises key questions: How do political, social, memory, and institutional factors influence historians' perspectives and preferences? Greek historiography in the past decades has focused more on social aspects of the 1940s conflict. Revisionist scholars favored micro approaches. This faced resistance, with accusations that postmodernism, anthropology, and oral history fragmented grand narratives into particularistic views of history.

Such commemorative rituals or ones of "cultural memorization" usually take place around monuments and memorials. These are primarily symbols located in a specific place. Nora (1989) claims that memory and history in the age of Modernity are contradictory, thus they are associated with different kinds of social spaces. The term *milieux de mémoire* refers to spaces and landscapes that embody memory as a lived experience, while history is related to the term *lieux de mémoire*, which refers to official places of memory (Nora, 1989). However, according to Papadakis et al. (2006, p. 15), an important reason why social spaces in their field of study, Cyprus, cannot be treated as either *lieux de mémoire* or *milieux de mémoire* but rather lie between the two concepts, is that many people have lived memories of the events that led to the current situation. Precisely for this reason, the usual way in which some people discuss history is as witnesses. The same can be said to apply to the events of 1940 in the field of research, especially with older informants.

Monuments are designed to act as a form of "punctuation" to the urban experience (Mubi Brighenti, 2010, p. 141). According to Mubi Brighenti (2010), the term "monument" derives from the Latin verb admŏnĕo (to admonish). As such, "the monument is the visible inscription of a public mnemonics" (Mubi Brighenti, 2010, p. 141). Brighenti "does not fully tease out the significance of this trace of the meaning of the monuments, however, in that they are meant to warn, dissuade and rebuke, as much as they are a state's attempt to create a heroic landmark in space and time" (Lloyd, 2022, p. 1). Numerous scholars have noted and illustrated the strong relationship between "monumental," culturally inscribed ambitions and national narratives (Harvey, 1985; Mitchell, 2003; Pred, 1995). Martínez (2022, p. 75) is right when pointing out that "monuments and memorials do not simply refer to a particular figure or historical period, but they are also a demonstration of power. In this sense, they not only have meaning by themselves, but also by their location, material condition and the resources mobilized by social elites for their construction and maintenance."

Politicization of memory has received much attention by social scientists, historians, art scholars, and more. Important work has demonstrated that memory is socially acquired, just as the past is social (Halbwachs, 1992 [1952]). As Mitchell (2003, p. 443) notes, "each age attempts to refashion and remake memory to serve its own contemporary purposes." Therefore, memory is deeply politicized. The interaction between communal remembering and repetition helps to maintain memory. Repetition is a key factor in blending the distinctions between different interpretations of the same events and producing a unified, highly idealized composite image during numerous memorial events and rituals. The generic social context for subsequent memories is therefore formed by this image, and as time passes, individual memories tend to fit into and match with this composite. (Mitchell, 2003). Connerton (1989) highlights the importance of public commemorations as a tool by which the nationalist narrative is injected into public memory. Such public commemorations, at least in rural Greece, usually take place around a memorial, such as the one under study. In most villages of Greece, there is a memorial in a central location, usually the village square, that commemorates the local "heroes," namely, those who have died in wartime. Even though "the memorialization of the dead with public monuments of some kind now seems natural and inevitable – an eternal practice" (Mitchell, 2003, p. 456), this form of public memorialization is a 19th century invention (Nora, 1989).

Summing up, one can say that monuments contribute to the strengthening of the historical, dominant memory in a community, but also to social cohesion, through the mechanisms of homogenization of the memory of its members, through commemorative rituals and events. Moreover, their very material nature and their presence in space are important to such processes. As Stavridis (1990, p. 115, my translation) notes:

> ...the essence of monumentality is indeed the condensation, through a not at all innocent abstraction of an event and its representation by the form of the monument. It is no coincidence that monuments are among the most powerful ways a society records its view of its history. The effectiveness of the imposition of the monuments is great, because their presence in the space gives them an empirically verifiable existence: They are there as proof of their truth.

This chapter sets off to examine transformations, perceived neglect, and contestations around the memorial under study. Based on ethnographic field research and observation of commemorations, interviews, as well as archival and bibliographical research, it attempts an archaeology of the memorial, by focusing on the ways in which the state imposed its national narrative(s) on the community and on the process of sense- and memory-making by the community as a response. This chapter does not claim as its novelty to argue that memory can be contentious and contested; however, it provides a case of alterations and neglect of memorializing materiality, as well as contestations that revolve around uses of space. It looks at how places of memory can demonstrate how the nation's conception has changed over time by examining the future of an existing memorial as Forest and Johnson (2002, p. 525) propose.

THE GREEK CIVIL WAR IN EPIRUS

Civil strife in Greece is often divided into three "rounds." The first one started in 1943, when the National Liberation Front (EAM), a communist-backed organization in Greece that fought the occupation, and its guerilla forces, the National People's Liberation Army (ELAS), occasionally found themselves engaging in combat with the National Republican Greek League, another resistance organization. Greece was in a crisis when it was liberated in October

1944, and another round of violence soon broke out as a result. A terror campaign supported by the government was initiated against EAM/ELAS members and supporters. The ELAS fighters withdrew to the highlands to engage in guerilla warfare. They changed their name to the DSE in December 1946. The newly installed communist governments of Albania, Bulgaria, and Yugoslavia supported the DSE. In September 1947 DSE switched from guerrilla to full-scale conventional military action. The GCW was not just a brutal internal conflict between two ideologically opposed Greek camps that were derogatively referred to as "monarcho-fascists" and "communist-bandits." The GCW served as the Allies' final opportunity to complete their agreements over the distribution of their wartime spoils. In January 1948, the siege of Konitsa by the DSE took place. Konitsa is in close proximity to Kefalovriso and the wider area was the theater of many battles and terror campaigns by both sides during the late 1940s. In late 1948, Yugoslavia had served as the DSE's primary training and supply base, but after the KKE sided with Stalin and denounced Tito (July 1949), the latter cut his military and logistical links with the DSE. Three months later, in the final DSE engagements on Greek soil, in the mountains of Grammos and Vitsi in Epirus and Macedonia, the communist forces were defeated.

After the GCW, there was a severe political division that resulted in the arrest and execution of tens of thousands of people. The rise of the military junta from 1967 to 1974 was the result of the country being ruled by a fervently right-wing, anti-communist military elite. Early in the 1980s, the center-left PASOK government allowed DSE veterans who had sought asylum in communist countries 30 years previously to return to Greece.

THE MEMORIAL IN KEFALOVRYSO

The memorial is situated in the central square of the Kefalovryso. The settlement is characterized both by its close proximity to the Greek-Albanian border, and by the bilingualism of the inhabitants (Greek – Vlach/Aromanian), who, until the middle of the 20th century, practiced transhumance, that is, nomadic animal husbandry (Alexakis, 2001). The village inhabitants would therefore spend half of the year close to the sea, mostly in the areas of Thesprotia and South East Albania, and half in Kefalovriso. It is a monument that seems to transform, on the one hand depending on the transformations in the ways the state's narratives regarding the memories of the GCW have changed, and on the other hand, based on the needs of the community members, causing contestations within the community on various levels.

The works for the erection of the memorial commenced in 1952 as a private initiative, after the community council decided to accept the donation of Sechis Sechopoulos from Vassiliko, a nearby settlement. The "Monument to the Victims of the [German] Occupation," as it was originally called, was created by Kostantinos Klouvatos (1923–2007), a well-known sculptor, and was unveiled in 1959. It was one of the first landscaping works in Greece, an artistic form introduced by Klouvatos and it has attracted interest by art critics: "K. Klouvatos introduced the concept of landscaping in the 1950s, by shaping exterior and interior spaces (monuments, squares, public spaces, and residences). In 1952, he carried out his first landscaping work in Kefalovryso of Epirus (Monument to the Victims of Occupation)" (Mortoglou, 2007, p. 12). Initially, it was decided as a memorial to the residents of Kefalovriso who were burned alive by the German Nazis of the Entelweiss division on July 10, 1943 (Fig. 7.1).

Fig 7.1. The Monument in Kefalovryso.

The Historical Event, and the Role of Language and Oral History

In his speech, Sechopoulos justified his donation by saying that "Kefalovriso offered sacrifices in the fight for freedom and this is why I decided to erect this monument. These people have their own language, but they wrote pages of Greek glory" (Mentis, 1997, p. 2). In his speech, he seems to recognize the otherness of the inhabitants of the settlement in relation to the rest of the settlements of the area, since it is the only Vlach-speaking village in the whole province of Pogoni, by noting that "these people have their own language," but at the same time includes them in the "homogeneous" national body, as they "offered sacrifices in the fight for freedom" and "wrote pages of Greek glory," in the standards imposed by nationalism, recognizing them in terms of national memory and history. Also, the word "but" is interesting, implying that they wrote pages of Greek glory, even though they have their own-different language.

The historical fact of the burning of the members of the community by the Germans, and the way it is represented in the collective oral memory of the community, is of great interest. According to Kourmantzi (2000, p. 2, my translation), a historian, the members of the community that were burned were not guerrillas and did not take part in the resistance, but simple herdsmen, a view that dovetails with the oral representations of the events by my interlocutors:

> ...the units are authorized and ordered in this struggle to take any measures, without restriction, either towards women or children, if [...] such measures are necessary for success. From our side, these horrible 'operations' become incomprehensible, as the Germans do not meet resistance from rebels in the villages that burn and execute civilians [...] At a first glance, it is most logical to attribute the executions that took place in those days in the villages of the area, including Kefalovryso to the ideology of the elite bodies of the German army [...] The tragedy of the case of the villages that suffered the greatest losses is that they could not know the Nazi worldview that had been passed on to the German army about the civilian population, that is, about ordinary people who had nothing to do with the war, and in these specific cases, there are not a few times when the village's dignitaries, out of naivety, not knowing the worldview they have to face, 'officially' welcome the Germans, only to be led shortly for execution, and in the worst case to be trapped in a building and burned there [...] With the entry of the German army into the village, some residents had stayed here, while a small reception was held. Among them, those who stayed in the village - as it is written - and would hand over the keys.

As mentioned above, this is a bilingual group and this fact has analytical and methodological implications, given that language is not only presupposing social structure and reality, but also creates them. Moreover, "language cannot be seen as transparent and innocent, but must be perceived as part of the relations of domination" (Tsitsipis, 2005, p. 102, my translation). Language is therefore an important and dynamic parameter of culture, playing a crucial role in social transformations, the reproduction of social structures, and so forth. In this case, the community's main marker of identity is language and importantly a spoken language with no written records that is not official in any nation-state. Given that an important element of any nation-state is a common language (Gellner, 2008) communities like this are interesting exceptions. In the genesis of the Greek nation as an imagined community (Anderson, 1983), national language, religion, and historiography constitute a hegemonic cultural front. In the case of Greek nationalism language has been instrumentalized as an important – if not the most important – cultural element. Lekas (1992, p. 141) notes that "there is perhaps no other criterion that so often and so completely declares the existence of a separate culture than language. It is therefore not surprising that linguistic specificity has been used more than any other distinguishing cultural feature to define the nation." The absence of a hegemonic state narrative in the Vlach language, the lack of words related to state policies, institutions and exercising power, and the use of Greek words in their place can lead to conclusions that concern not only the language, but also social structures in general and memory in particular.

To illustrate how the above are relevant in this case, an indicative excerpt from an interview with K.K., a retired worker is presented, in which he constantly switches from one language to the other:

> …*[in Greek] You should have seen that. Kachrimanis [the prefecture governor], the marshal, they all came here from Ioannina. People? Phew… Packed. They talked about about those who were burned alive… You know, that guy, M. has [written] a poem. Very nice. It is called heroes.*
>
> *Q. Did you have any of your own among them?*
>
> *A. [in Vlach] How could I not have; my grandfather was there. If you go there, his name is written. He was here [pointing to his house], I remember that day. He said I will go down [to the village center] to see what is going on, because someone said they are gathering the people. What was I back then? A baby. And [my] mother told him: Wow, black fated, where are you going, sit down,*

where are you going, they are going to kill you. Don't be afraid, they won't kill me he said and laughed. And, they burned him…

Within the narration, the same event is presented at first as a heroic act that needs to be celebrated representing the victims as heroes, but in the interlocutor's individual and family memory, his grandfather in no way expected what was bound to happen. In fact, the whole event is represented as something accidental and the man as ignoring any risk, unable to imagine he was walking to his torturous death. This representation contradicts the narrative of the hero that later prevailed, which was also mediated and promoted by the Greek state and the commemorative rituals around the memorial. In general, references to the event correspond to a mediated narrative and the memory of the event is not uniform across narratives by the same person, let alone by different members of the community. Interestingly, when my interlocutors recounted incidents from the war, they spoke in Greek, which can be explained with reference to the inadequacy of the Vlach language in articulating an official national language. Moreover, when speaking Greek, they are often reproducing official state narratives about the World War II (WW2) and the GCW.

The recounts concerning the burning of the community members are of two kinds: Some that are always in Greek and reproduce the official narrative, enriched with references to the commemorative ceremony that takes place every year and involves the laying of wreaths at the memorial. Usually, these narratives include references to the guests of honor and their capacities, but leave aside the historical event as recorded in the oral memory of the community. The second category of narratives is articulated in the Vlach language and refers to the people executed, not as heroes, but as members of the community. The memory of the community appears parallel to the national without intersecting, given that the two narratives are often incompatible with each other or even contradictory. In general, the use of Vlach language reflects the collective memory of the group and the individual and family memory of its members, while the use of Greek language reflects the national, official memory.

The event of July 1943 is also recorded in the local oral tradition, through a polyphonic song, the lyrics of which commemorate the executed (my translation from Vlach): "In the year of 43, what a great destruction found Kefalovryso/Cry Kefalovryso cry because you were drowned in blood/ Saturday midday terror hit upon us/Get out, you men, do not let the jinxed village burn/Hey friends, death found us, the machine gun is boiling in the village/They gathered them one by one in two houses and locked them in/They set fire to their door, they all grabbed hold of each other/The priest with the liturgy in the pocket, the poor men must be thirsty/Come friends let us kiss, kiss and part/because in the next life we will meet each other/As the raider left who can recognize Lambris Simos/They all scream together for Ilias, son of Giorgakis Mentis/The horses are waiting to load the cheese, who can recognize Giorgos Bassios/The house burned and the wall fell, who recognizes Belos Kouros/The red slope turned black, who knows Nikolakis Gintosias/Who could this be, he is like Christos Demiris/My village a great evil found you, you also lost your secretary."

In the song, the victims are represented as ordinary people, while references are made to their lives and professions. Also, emphasis is placed on the event itself, without mentioning what preceded or followed or the wider war that was raging across Greece at the time. Another song that was written later in the 1950s offers an interesting contrast. This song, also in Vlach, is called "Mijidei Vrute" (Beloved Kefalovryso), written by Nikos Natsias, a community member and referring to the WW2, but also to the burning of the community members in 1943, as evident in the following selected lyrics: "Beloved Kefalovriso, you were so fine/In 1940 the year looked very bad/The Italian came to us and then the German/The whole village was burned down, the bazaar broke down/A great slaughter [happened], we threw them into the sea/Many airplanes, covered the sun/poor Greece."[1] In this case, we see how the second song does not refer to the victims separately, but to the village as a whole, integrating it into the wider nation (poor Greece), with references to war and occupation, but also to the victory of the Greek Army (we threw them into the sea).

Materiality of Memory: The Memorial

The memorial in its original form consisted of a central marble column, the visual subject of which is human figures engulfed in flames, with a figure of a priest standing out, while at its base is an inscribed reference:

AND WITH THE CROWD I BECAME ONE BODY
ONE GIANT BODY
THAT BREATHES HOT AIR AND WILD FIRE FAR AWAY
BEHIND OUR BROKEN WALLS
FREEDOM
THIS MONUMENT WAS ERECTED BY STAVROS SECHIS SECHOPOULOS

The visual subject is a direct reference to the burning of the residents of the settlement in July 1943 by the German army. The memorial involves eight more marble columns, four on each side of the centerpiece, on which the names of the executed are listed. An issue that begs for noting is which names are written where and in what way. Initially, on the marble slabs, not only the names of those killed in the incident of July 1943 were included, but there was also another slab titled "murdered...," with the rest of the title being ineligible, as well as two others that are titled "executed..." again with the rest of the title being ineligible, due to the fact that these titles no longer exist today, as they were chiseled out. According to my interlocutors, they were referring to the so-called bandit war [συμμοριτοπόλεμο] and included casualties of the GCW, victims of the so-called communist bandits. In this initial form of the monument, the dominant ideology at the time with its intense anti-communist rhetoric is prevalent, given that "the victors are dominant in most post conflict environments, and Greece was to be no exception to this rule" (Siani-Davies & Katsikas, 2009, p. 563).

References to the "gang war" are not unique in this case. They are also found in other monuments in the wider area of Konitsa as Giannopoulou and Kouros (2012) note, usually in monuments erected during the first two decades after the GCW. The proximity of the settlement to the Greek-Albanian border, in an area that has been the theater of many battles in the GCW, is also important, as Dalkavoukis and Drinis (2009, p. 67) argue about the same wider area:

> *In a field of intense confrontations and wars, it is normal that places of memory primarily concern the winners. In this context, the decade of the 1940s includes two military conflicts in the region, the Greco-Italian War, as an episode of World War II, and the Civil War. In both cases the final winner was the view identified with the nation-state, against either the external or the internal enemy. This logic seems to greatly manipulate the expressions of collective memory and its presence in the landscape.*

The design of the memorial is also of great interest, since in the slabs entitled "Burned Alive," there is a distinction. Although the two slabs could fit all the names of those executed, there is a third, eponymous one, in which only two names are listed. A drifter from Corfu and the village priest, who were also burned along with the rest. What differentiates them, however, is that they were not Vlachs, therefore Others. This differentiation as reflected in the monument highlights the existence of another division apart from the national one (Greeks–Germans) and the political one (Leftists–Rightists); that of the Vlach ethnic identity of the inhabitants. Much could be said here about the Self and Other that would however exceed both the ambition and the scope of this chapter. What can be said is that there is an ethnic distinction, which is reflected in the spatial organization of the memorial.

The memorial was originally merely a part of the wider landscape art piece by Klouvatos. The latter initially occupied the area of the entire village square, together with landscaped gardens, a fountain and more elements. Also, in the area around the memorial, from the time it was inaugurated, all commemorations took place, with the laying of wreaths by the local school pupils, war veterans, and so on. As highlighted previously, rituals of this kind contribute to the consolidation of a collective identification between participants on two levels: On the one hand, at the national level, since they always refer to the nation emphasizing the common struggles and common interests of its citizens. On the other hand, they also contribute to the cohesion between the members of the community.

The "Adventures" of the Memorial

What is clearly of interest in this chapter "is not just the original constructions of these innumerable commemorative sites of collective memory, but the contemporary struggles over the *transformation* of these old markers and their associated meanings: the rewriting of history and memory and the translations of the past" (Mitchell, 2003, p. 448). After 1981, when the dominant political ideology in the Greek national state was expressed by PASOK (Panhellenic Socialist Movement) which formed a government at that time, the dominant narratives and practices pertaining to WW2 and the GCW changed radically. The main feature of this party was a mixture of nationalism and socialism that merged a socialist strategy with a nationalist strategy (Sassoon, 1996).

On an ideological level, this change was reflected in the so-called national reconciliation, but also in the institutional recognition of the National Resistance (1982). According to Siani-Davies and Katsikas (2009, p. 568):

> *The main PASOK slogan was 'change,' but the term 'reconciliation' also featured in the speeches of party leaders. For Papandreou and the other leaders of PASOK, 'reconciliation' meant coming to terms with the past by wiping the slate clean. The whole of the recent history of Greece was to be reappraised. The anticommunist triumphalism of the right, the foundation stone upon which the post-1945 Greek state had been built, was to be overturned and the role of the left re-evaluated, so*

as to bring an end to the discrimination which had excluded large segments of Greek society from public life.

This shift in the state narrative marked the recognition by the official state of the victims of both warring sides, aiming at national cohesion and homogeneity. Indicative of this shift was the consolidation in that period of concepts such as civil strife, fratricidal war, and others, which were used to characterize the civil war. It is also the time when the left-wing community of memory begins to become present in various aspects of social, political, and artistic life.

Regarding the Kefalovryso memorial, the 1980s and the shift described earlier are crucial, in that it is the period in which disputes about the memorial are openly expressed and a long period of transformations commences. Indeed, politics of memory take center stage at times of significant political disjuncture, according to Forest and Johnson (2002, p. 525). In such times, monuments in particular turn into hotbeds of intense contention. The analysis of places of memory, the authors hold, "provides an ideal way to uncover underlying continuities and discontinuities in national identity politics." In the case of Kefalovryso, in the community council minutes numbered 6/1983, a relevant proposal of the president, elected with the support of PASOK, is recorded:

> *I propose that July 10 of each year, starting from this year, be declared a holiday in our community, because on this day in the year 1943, residents of our community were burned alive by the Germans, and also that some titles be deleted from the inscriptions that exist in today's memorial, which cause division among our people, such as the title "murdered by the communist gangs" and the placement of a slab (inscription) with the title "fallen Kefalovrysites as a result of the First and Second World War and the Asia Minor War" and to add the other names of the fallen, and called the council to decide on it.*

What is important about the above quote is the attempt to transform the monument in an attempt to align with the standards of the shift in narratives on the GCW at the national/government level. The president of the community, as a representative of this new narrative, also uses its vocabulary. The reference he makes to "our people" is indicative, apparently referring to the Greek people as a whole.

A direct transfer of the dominant ideology to the local level, through the community leader is observed. The local society as part of the wider national social formation cannot remain unaffected by the conditions set by the national ideology. This means the adaptation of locality to the demands of national homogeneity, a process in which both memory and the reconstruction of the past are important elements. The abovementioned decision of the community council was in line with the proposals of the central policy of that period as described above. The decision and implementation of the changes to the monument make it a palimpsest monument. The term palimpsest in its literal version is used to describe the repeated writing of texts on the same parchment. In its metaphorical use, the elements that make up the culturally determined use of the space are perceived as texts or inscriptions, while the "parchment" is the space itself. Also, although the president mentions the world wars and the Asia Minor war, he does not mention the civil war at all, despite the fact that many of the names that existed before, as well as those that he proposes to add, are names of fallen of both fronts of the civil war.

Eventually, the title in question was erased with a chisel, the marks of which are still visible today, and two more marble slabs were added, under the general title "Fallen in World War II." But even this transformation has been a field of contestations, disputes, and controversies between community members. Several of my informants particularly emphasized their disagreement with the decision of the community council at the time, one of which told me "in the memorial only the names of those who were burned should be written and all the rest could be in a separate monument." In addition, an article in the local newspaper (Porikis, 2000, p. 3, my translation from Greek) states that:

> ...the memorial was falsified by adding other names that had nothing to do with the history of the memorial. I respect the history of these people, but a separate memorial could be built in their honor.

The civil war is still today a field of controversy. It is worth noting that even though there was a reference to the civil war through the monument in its initial form (killed by the communist sympathizers), my informants seemed to ignore it and identify the previous form of the monument only with those executed in July 1943.

In Theodoros Maragos' film, "Learn letters, my child," the plot unfolds in a village in Arcadia shortly after the dictatorship period, which ended in 1974. The unveiling of a memorial to those who fell during the German Occupation upsets and causes strife in the local community, as the name of Christos Kanavos, a communist resistance guerrilla who was killed in the area, is omitted. The film tackles one of the issues that concerns this chapter, the controversy over how a community remembers the Occupation period and the Civil War. The fact that such disputes took place in many areas Greece, as can be seen both from ethnographic examples and the film, may allow a certain generalization of the conclusions of this chapter.

Another alteration to the memorial took place in 1983, when the square where the monument was located, was reconstructed, again following a decision of the community council. This once again created disagreements and disputes among the members of the community. An excerpt from the local newspaper is illuminating:

> *As long as the children of heroes lived and controlled the fortune of the village, the flag of honor was held high. Since their grandkids took over, then nothing. Year after year, the holocaust, the honoring of heroes became a chore, degraded to the point where it bordered on irreverence. We, the descendants, without a trace of respect, sacrificed our grandparents, once again on the altar of a larger square that looks like the Bridge of Arta, it is made, made again and has no fixing. We dislodged the heroes and set them up naked at the edge of a bleak square. Whoever does not honor his past and his traditions, does not honor himself, does not know where he came from, who he is and where he is going. That's it, enough is enough! [We need] To restore the memory and honor of our heroes, like they deserve, because we will not be worthy to be called Kefalovrysites. It is necessary, immediately, to form a space similar to the one we destroyed and to transfer there the souls of our heroes, because they are not going to rest as long as they are in this ice-cold corner, among bouzouki, cifteteli dance and Militses.*
> *(Mentis, 1997, p. 2, my translation from Greek)*

Katherine Verdery (1999), refers to the "political life of dead bodies." In the passage above, the author does the same, through a highly emotional speech, talking about the "souls of our heroes" and memory. He even considers the latter a cohesive element between past, present, and future. Indeed, the past can legitimize the present situation. The members of a social group have a common memory as a basic condition. When shared memory is absent, intergenerational communication is hindered, as generations are unable to share experiences and conclusions (Connerton, 1989). Todorova (2004) titles her introduction to her book titled "Balkan Identities," "Learning Memory, Remembering Identity." This title, reversing the expected phrase, shows the almost natural correlation of these two concepts on the one hand, and the plasticity of memory on the other. Issues concerning collective memory are to some extent related to those concerning identity, precisely because there can be no collective identity without collective memory.

Monuments and memorials are first and foremost symbols in space and place. The contested spatial aspect of the monument is highlighted in yet another piece in the local newspaper:

> *The years have passed, the conditions have improved, the needs of the residents have changed. The place was filled up, the monument was moved without planning, and with carelessness to its current location. The surprising thing is that the memorial was eliminated in favor of the popular traditional feast. (Porikis, 2000, p. 3, my translation)*

On the one hand, many of my interlocutors expressed the opinion that it was wrong to alter the space of the square, on the other hand, a portion of residents believe that there was a practical necessity for a place where the annual village feast will be held. The president of the community at the time the decision was made to alter the square, told me: "the community authority decided that the needs of the village were to have a place to hold the annual festival." It is interesting that the members of the community who live permanently in the village, supported more the second point of view, while those who live in urban centers and visit the village usually in their summer vacation, the first. This dispute about space also reveals a cultural dispute. On the one hand the so-called high culture, emphasizing the aesthetic value of the artistic work, on the other a "low" traditional culture, highlighting the need for a space that can facilitate the annual feast. Such feasts in the context of traditional societies performed very important functions, as they not only relieved the members of the community from their heavy workload, but at the same time played a decisive role in maintaining social cohesion among its members (Dalkavoukis, 2005, pp. 102–103, my translation).

In this case, there is a reverse process to the previous ones: While in the previous transformations of the monument, the dominant state ideology played a primary role, in this one the community itself, according to its needs, transforms the space, so that it becomes more functional and caters to its needs. The memorial eventually changed several positions within the area of the square until it was placed where it is today. Even the sculptor himself, was allegedly displeased by the alteration of his work, according to some of my interlocutors.

CONCLUSION

The concept of memory is very often related to that of identity, in particular the concept of "dominant, historical memory" with that of national identity: "The parallel lives of these concepts alert us to the fact that the concept of identity is based on the idea of memory and vice versa" (Gillis, 1996, p. 3). In other words, these are interdependent terms, which are dynamic, that is, subject to transformations. This chapter followed the contemporary struggles over the transformations of a memorial and the associated meanings of these transformations: "the rewriting of history and memory and the translations of the past" (Mitchell, 2003, p. 448). The "adventures" of the memorial in the second half of the 20th century reflect to an extent the "adventures" of the social memory and forgetting of the community. All the controversies, disagreements and claims I described do not simply concern space in its material dimensions, but also the symbols that define it. As Mitchell (2003, p. 448) eloquently notes, "the traces of memory left in the landscape point to the political, cultural and economic forces which cohered at that moment to produce a vision of the way a (dominant) society perceived and represented itself to itself."

NOTE

1. Mijidei is the old name of Kefalovryso, before it was renamed by the government in the 1930s. This was part of a wider policy by the Greek state to eliminate toponyms of "foreign" origins.

REFERENCES

Alexakis, E. (2001). Εθνοτικές Ομάδες, Πόλεμος και Ιστορική Μνήμη στους Έλληνες Βλάχους του Κεφαλοβρύσου (Μετζιντιέ) Πωγωνίου [Ethnic groups, war and historical memory among the Greek Vlachs of Kefalovriso (Mitsintie) Pogoniou]. *Ethnologia*, (No 9). Αθήνα.

Althusser, L. (2010). Ideology and ideological state apparatuses (notes towards an investigation) (1970). In *Cultural theory: An anthology*. Verso.

Anderson, B. (1983). *Imagined communities: Reflections on the origin and spread of nationalism*. Verso books.

Antoniou, G. (2007). The lost Atlantis of objectivity: The revisionist struggles between the academic and public spheres 1. *History and Theory*, 46(4), 92–112.

Bal, M., Crewe, J. V., & Spitzer, L. (Eds.). (1999). *Acts of memory: Cultural recall in the present*. Upne.

Connerton, P. (1989). *How societies remember*. Cambridge University Press.

Dalkavoukis, V. (2005). Η Πένα και η Γκλίτσα [*The pen and the shepherd's crook*]. Odysseas.

Dalkavoukis, V., & Drinis, Y. (2009). Κατανοώντας το παλίμψηστο του τόπου: ευθείες και πλάγιες συνδηλώσεις σε ένα συνοριακό τοπίο [Understanding the palimpsest of place: Direct and indirect connotations in a border landscape]. In M. Spyridakis (Ed.), Μετασχηματισμοί του χώρου: κοινωνικές και πολιτισμικές διαστάσεις [*Transformations of space: Social and cultural aspects*]. Nisos.

Forest, B., & Johnson, J. (2002). Unraveling the threads of history: Soviet-Era monuments and Post-Soviet national identity in Moscow. *Annals of the Association of American Geographers*, 92(3), 524–547.

Gellner, E. (2008). *Nations and nationalism*. Cornell University Press.

Giannopoulou, C., & Kouros, T. (2012). Τοπία άμυνας απέναντι σε ένα 'διπλό εχθρό'. Μνημεία του στρατού για τη δεκαετία του 1940 στην περιοχή της Κόνιτσας [Landscapes of defense against a 'double enemy.' Army monuments of the army about the 1940s in the Konitsa region]. In V. Dalkavoukis, E. Paschaloudi, N. Skoulidas, & K. Tsekou (Eds.), *Narratives on the 1940s*. Epikentro.

Gillis, J. R. (ed.). (1996). *Commemorations: The politics of national identity*. Princeton University Press.

Halbwachs, M. (1992). *On collective memory*. University of Chicago press.

Harvey, D. (1985). The geopolitics of capitalism. *Social Relations and Spatial Structures*, 126, 128–163.

Iggers, G. G. (2009). A search for a post-postmodern theory of history [Review of meaning and representation in history, by J. Rüsen]. *History and Theory*, 48(1), 122–128.

Koliopoulos, J. S., & Veremis, T. M. (2009). *Modern Greece: A history since 1821*. John Wiley & Sons.

Kourmantzi, E. (2000, July). Κεφαλόβρυσο (Μετζιτιέ), το πρώτο μαρτυρικό χωριό της Ηπείρου [Kefalovryso (Metsintie), the first martyr village of Epirus]. *Pigi Kefalovrisou*.

Kouros, T. (2016). Παραχάραξη ή Δικαίωση; Η διεκδίκηση της Συλλογικής Μνήμης και του Χώρου μέσα από ένα Παλίμψηστο Μνημείο [Misrepresentation or justification? Claiming memory and place through a palimpsest memorial]. *Ethnologia Online*. 4/2016. https://doi.org/10.5281/zenodo.7693302

Lekas, P. (1992). *Εθνικιστική Ιδεολογία* [Nationalist ideology]. Mnimon.

Lloyd, J. (2022). Monuments and the sited struggles of memorialisation. *Space and Culture*, 25(2), 341–344. https://doi.org/10.1177/1206331221990947

Martínez, F. (2022). Memory, don't speak! Monumental neglect and memorial sacrifice in contemporary Estonia. *Cultural Geographies*, 29(1), 63–81. https://doi.org/10.1177/14744740211005517

Mentis, M. (1997, December). ΟΛΟΚΑΥΤΩΜΑ – στα όρια της ασέβειας [HOLOCAUST – Bordering disrespect]. *Pigi Kefalovrisou*, 2.

Mitchell, K. (2003). Monuments, memorials, and the politics of memory. *Urban Geography*, 24(5), 442–459.

Mortoglou, I. (2007). Εργο ωραίο και αληθινό, Σαράντα μέρες συμπληρώθηκαν από το θάνατο του Κώστα Κλουβάτου [Work beautiful and true, 40 days after the passing of Kostas Klouvatos]. *Rizospastis*. https://www.rizospastis.gr/page.do?publDate=24%2F6%2F07&pageNo=4&id=8705. Accessed on June 24, 2007.

Mubi Brighenti, A. (2010). At the wall: Graffiti writers, urban territoriality, and the public domain. *Space and Culture*, 13(3), 315–332.

Nora, P. (1989). Memory and history. *Les Lieux de Mémoire Representations*, 26, 7.

Papadakis, Y. (2003). Nation, narrative and commemoration: Political ritual in divided Cyprus. *History and Anthropology*, 14(3), 253–270.

Papadakis, Y., Peristianis, N., & Welz, G. (2006). Introduction: Modernity, history, and conflict in divided Cyprus: An overview. In *Divided Cyprus: Modernity, history, and an island in conflict* (pp. 2–29). Indiana University Press.

Poole, R. (2008). Memory, history and the claims of the past. *Memory Studies*, *1*(2), 149–166.

Porikis, I. (2000, January). Μνήμες και Ερωτήματα [Memories and questions]. *Pigi Kefalovrisou*, 3.

Poster, M. (1984). *Foucault, Marxism and history mode of production versus mode of information.* Blackwell.

Pred, A. (1995). Out of bounds and undisciplined: Social inquiry and the current moment of danger. *Social Research*, 1065–1091.

Ricoeur, P. (2006). Memory – Forgetting – History. In J. Rüsen (Ed.), *Meaning and representation in history* (Vol. 7). Berghahn Books.

Sassoon, D. (1996). *100 years of socialism: The west European left in the twentieth century.* IB Tauris.

Siani-Davies, P., & Katsikas, S. (2009). National reconciliation after civil war: The case of Greece. *Journal of Peace Research*, *46*(4), 559–575.

Stavridis, S. (1990). *η Συμβολική Σχέση με τον Χώρο* [*The symbolic relation to Space*]. Kalvos.

Todorova, M. (2004). *Balkan identities: Nation and memory.* NYU Press.

Tsitsipis, L. (2005). *Από τη Γλώσσα ως Αντικείμενο στη Γλώσσα ως Πράξη* [*From language as object to language as act*]. Nisos.

Verdery, K. (1999). *The political lives of dead bodies: Reburial and postsocialist change.* Columbia University Press.

8

DIGITALLY MEDIATED COLLECTIVE MEMORY OF THE GREEK CIVIL WAR: A POST-MEMORY ANALYSIS OF YOUTUBE COMMENTS

LEANDROS SAVVIDES[a] AND IOANNA FERRA[b]

[a]University of Cyprus, Cyprus
[b]HSE University, Russia

Keywords: Digitally mediated memory; pastiche; post-memory; Greek Civil War; digital platforms

INTRODUCTION

This study investigates the depiction of digitally mediated memory in the digital context, focusing on analysis of YouTube videos and comments for the case of the Greek Civil War (1940s). The study explores YouTube as an indicative example of the digital media manifestation of technological infrastructure shaping collective remembrance and forgetting of conflict. YouTube here is used as an indicative example of digital media, that illustrates how collective remembrance is shaped through two different, yet complementary paths: first, it provides an alternative space for production and reproduction of memory (as seen through users' engagement and comments), and secondly, it provides an example of digitization of archive (as regarding the actual video posted).

Digital platforms, including YouTube, operate as a spectacular space where historical videos are consumed as commodities and cultural reproduction. The form and content are tailored to fit within the parameters set by the spectacle of digital media, catering to the dynamics of online attention, engagement metrics, and algorithmic recommendations, evident by the affective nature of user engagement. Therefore, the impact that platforms affordances and algorithms might have on shaping digitally mediated memory indicates risks regarding erasing or marginalizing voices and perspectives, facilitating the manipulation and distortion of historical content. The discussion is situated within the debate that perceives the proliferation of such digital and online media on the one hand as further democratization of public space and, on the other hand, as manifestations and symptoms of sociotechnical infrastructure and cultural reproduction in late capitalism. Consequently, we would like to pose a question that we can hardly answer in this chapter: how do developments in sociotechnical infrastructure and the prevalence of digital media in everyday life contribute to the fragmentation and recombination of historical narratives – or in other words, the loss of historicity? (Gkotzaridis, 2011; Van Dijck, 2007). We do not content to unearth the question of structure versus agency or present a mechanistic view of cultural reproduction; however, we do aim to discuss media as part of the discussion about history, particularly for Greece, and the uses and misuses of collective memory about critical events that shape political action to this day.

It is important to note that an earlier version of this chapter is published at the edited volume *Class, Culture, and the Media in Greece* (Mylonas & Psyllakou, 2024), emphasizing the role of class as it appears in Greek media. In this more recent version, the study emphasized on the association of digital media to memory, the notion of post-memory in relation to the historical context of the examined case, while the analysis of the collected data concentrated on detecting discourses as seen in a transnational, national, and individual context. Moving to the conclusion, this chapter makes a reference to the question of cultural reproduction memory, a consideration only partially answered here, and is yet to researched, looking on the analyzed data set in juxtaposition and comparison to other YouTube videos (content and comments).

DIGITAL MEDIA AND DIGITALLY MEDIATED PAST

The study of the construction of digitally mediated collective memory should be situated into the wider debate regarding digital media, their affordances, and the impact to contemporary societies and the everyday life (Hoskins, 2018). Memory and remembrance, and also their association with the media, is a fruitful field of inquiry that touches upon various theoretical arguments and questions of representation, digitization of archive, collective memory, and mediated memory, and, ultimately, history. Focusing on digital media, key terms and concepts, such as "platformization" and memory, "datafication" of the everyday life (and in extend memory), and the broader questions focusing on data, point to some of the most recent debates in the field, regarding the commodification of life, including the "personal and collective past" – data as memories and vice versa (Locatelli, 2021; Pangrazio & Selwyn, 2023; Smit et al., 2024).

In this context, the frames in which the datafication process evolves are shaped according to the affordances of the platform per se and, therefore, within the structures in which the platform is designed to achieve commercial benefits. Therefore, digital infrastructure is another variable and a site of contention about history and collective memory between various actors, institutional and individual users alike. The platform provides a space for individuals to engage and be turned into dividuals, forming networked and algorithmic publics (Boyd, 2010; Livingstone, 2005). This highlights the gap between the collective subject of the Marxist tradition – where the individual understands their identity in relation to their class – and the individual as a rational subject within the liberal tradition. Additionally, it contrasts with the "dividual," a consumer subject that functions as an unconscious assemblage of statistical data processed by algorithms (Goriunova, 2019). While the Marxist tradition emphasizes the collective, as a way of approaching history, as political subjects (mediated by organizations/party); on the other hand, the liberal tradition emphasizes the individual citizen (mediated by the civil society) (Fritsch, 2006; Funkenstein, 1989; Lukacs, 2017). Networks features define the way that individuals will form publics, and these publics will later be reshaped by algorithms (McKelvey, 2014). The networked publics that are turned to algorithmic publics might be invisible, emerge in collapsed contexts, not having full control over content and function according to temporalities of technology. That result to the further dispute of publics as democratic agents (Lippmann, 1997). Publics though are figurative and reassemble according to algorithms functions, whereas the individual is now understood as the dividual (McKelvey, 2014).

The tradition of digitally mediated past and post-memory is now increasingly surpassed by the notion of dividuality (mediated by commercially driven algorithmic assemblages), which discards reflexivity for affect and experience and which resembles scattered traces of algorithmic identity based on the movement of an individual on the internet (McKelvey, 2014). The black box of algorithmically driven classifications and statistical data filter what and how we see, expose, and engage to online information and the digital world

(Pariser, 2014), creating algorithmic identities and impressionable subjects, and thus, ultimately, also shape the way we engage with information as data and in extend history. To this end, Gillespie (2014) argues that – internet – platforms do not only mediate as much as they constitute (virtual and fragmented) what appears to be public discourse. Additionally, what is often presented as raw data in digital media is an oxymoron term (Gitelman & Jackson, 2013), and the technical infrastructure and tools do shape the arguments and point to its limits. In other words, tools and affordances utilized to discuss history contain political and relations of production themselves. This argument is, we believe, a continuity to the 20th century discussion that was evident about form and content in literary circles (Jameson, 2015).

Networks and algorithms result to mechanism of what Jameson (2015) discussed as spatialization of memory, referring to the ways in which memory and historical consciousness are organized and structured in space. In the digital age – and space – memory is increasingly mediated and shaped within digital technologies, leading to new forms of spatialization and organization. Digital media provided new spatial frameworks for the storage, retrieval, and dissemination of memory and historical information (Carbajal & Caswell, 2021). Therefore, the spatialization of memory within the digital media environment is formulated reflecting the key features and limitations of digital media affordances. That includes the nonlinear organization of memory, the fragmentation and recombination of memory and context, the global accessibility, and the virtuality of information (Boyd, 2010; McKelvey, 2014).

The nonlinear organization of memory draws from the nonhierarchical and rhizomatic networks through which information flows. Similarly, memory is now produced/reproduced in spatial distributed and interconnected networks, enabling nonlinear narratives and multiple entry points into historical and cultural content. Digital media facilitate the fragmentation and recombination of memory and historical content, allowing the juxtaposition of diverse historical elements and narratives (Hoskins, 2009, 2018). Next, in this mode of organization of memory, digital media bypass physical limitations, providing access to a wide range of historical and cultural content from diverse geographic locations, allowing for the global circulation and dissemination of memory. Finally, digital technologies enable the creation of virtual and augmented reality environments that organize memory in immersive and interactive ways (Challenor & Ma, 2019), allowing the recreation and reimagining of historical spaces and events, and in extend, memory experiences.

Reflecting on digital media debates regarding participation, democracy, and so on, this mode of memory spatialization could be considered as promoting the "democratization of access to historical and cultural content," enabling diverse voices and perspectives to be represented and shared. On the other hand, it raises questions about the authenticity, curation, and preservation of memory in digital spaces, as well as concerns about the potential for manipulation and distortion of historical narratives. Considering that algorithms and their functionality is usually termed as a "black box" (Christin, 2020) difficult to crack (mostly because most algorithms are developed by private companies; hence, they are commercial secrets and source of competitive advantage), audit studies have been gaining some interest in attempts to reverse engineer websites, platforms, and applications, pointing on issues of transparency, bias, and so on (Vecchione et al., 2021).

For example, Makhortykh et al. (2021) audited the curation of Google on how it curates the visual representation of the Holocaust. By engaging with the user experience and working on the variations of recommendations of the platform, audit studies try to understand the ranking and thus argue on the level of distortion of a historical event based on the search results. Such distortion can result in trivialization and revisionism, thus shaping political perceptions and actions. Visual representation is important as the user views an articulation of a historical event through emotionally intense experience, similar to the curation of images in a museum (Hansen-Glucklich, 2014). The difference of algorithmic curation is that it considers commercially exploited clicks of the impressionable subject (the dividuaded subject) – instead of being a conscious decision that can be discussed and subjected to scrutiny and criticism (MacKenzie & Porter, 2019). Thus, a historical event as traumatic as the Holocaust is, in this context, mediated for commercial purposes instead of providing space for social intercourse, on accepting and processing the actual event. This process does not set political-related questions, and it is rather instrumentalized for the commercial interest as shaped by the algorithmic mediator (owned by a private company). That is having a significant impact of the fragmentation and detachment of information from a theoretical basis and subsumption of method to an extra-social nonreflexive process.

Despite the question regarding human agency on the production of audiovisual material, technology in the form of algorithmically mediated audiovisual narratives is the one that increasingly shapes the frames in which the memory is transferred from one generation to the next. This is a relatively new area of inquiry, given the proliferation of media and data studies in the past decade, looking at the relationship between political ideologies and historical events when examined via digital methods (see, for example, Schneider, 2018). Online platforms are business models that feed on user engagement. As such, affordances are an important part for guiding and suggesting paths of action of users. Thus, many discussions center on technical affordances and how they shape discourse around historical phenomena, influencing human agency by defining contemporary modes of communication. Others suggest an emancipatory reading of these media technologies (O'Sullivan, 2011), mainly emphasizing on the decentralization of authorship and thus, in a state of becoming, new ways of reading, by traversing readers through hyperlinks, alongside to the availability of access to a wider public. Despite highlighting the illusion of technology as being responsible and able in creating a totalizing knowledge (O'Sullivan, 2011), what usually remains outside the discussion is the creation of media habits that essentially influence the way history is consumed and, by extension, understood. In this sense, the mediated history is composed of fragments of "collapsing complexities" (Schneider, 2018, p. 430).

POST-MEMORY AND HISTORICAL CONTEXT

During the advent of the 21st century, Greece had already been through the Metapolitefsi period by some time, experiencing a center-left government that was attempting to cut the social democratic politics from economic regulations, essentially accepting the Western affiliation of the country (*aneikomen sti dysi*) and the "end of history" narrative. Hadjivassiliou (2018) noted that in the battle for collective memory about the Greek Civil War, there was a renewed interest within literature circles during the early 2000s, as a new generation of writers, often fiction writers, attempted to understand and reconstruct the past through storytelling. This is also in accordance with developments both nationally and at an international level. It can be seen as part of the proliferation and development of the memory and novel industry within the country (as a way of narrating history in contrast to partisan politics), as much as the distance to the historical events. Having separated history from frameworks and perceptual tools in terms of material conditions toward the concept of memory and oral history, what remains is a battlefield for the politics of memory (Danforth & Van Boeschoten, 2019). Therefore, linking to the concept of post-memory, Hirsch (2012) explains that:

> ...*the relationship that the 'generation after' bears to the personal, collective, and cultural trauma of those who came before-to experiences they 'remember' only by means of the stories, images, and behaviors among which they grew up. But these experiences were transmitted to them so deeply and affectively as to seem to constitute memories in their own right. Postmemory's connection to*

> *the past is thus actually mediated not by recall but by imaginative investment, projection, and creation. (Hirsch, 2012, p. 5)*

In his recent book, Alvanos (2022) attempts to understand the readers of history, by constructing narratives of the historical events based on the "rival identities" (sic). Similarly, Marantzidis (2013) in his latest book discussed the commitment of communists as religious in nature, for not abandoning their cause after the fall of the Soviet Union. In both examples, the authors assert that history, like most things, is a social construction; therefore, the task is to carefully choose information and knowledge, which will contribute on accepting past historical contentions and trauma. History in this sense is a matter of cultural appropriation, a flexible topic that can be shaped according to political ends, without judgment of either side. Marantzidis contends that through memory, Civil War is often utilized by political actors for political marketing (communication) purposes, in a process very similar to what Hirsch (2012) refers to as post-memory.

> *Most of those who lived through the Civil War have passed away. What exists is a postmemory. It's not direct experience, but 'I've heard, I've read, I think it happened that way'. I've seen it on my tours of National Reconciliation Park on the Gramos; people for whom the Civil War was, really, a strong part of their identity, their family history, which redirected them toward certain political factions. (Marantzidis, 2023)*

Of course, such social constructionist and highly relativist approaches see post-memory as a potential tool that could heal societal factions and polarization; they read history as part of traumatic experiences. In contrast, materialist conceptions of history emphasize in historical accuracy and truth (Navickas, 2018), conceptualizing history through the prism of antagonistic forces that subject political circumstances, heating up and even end in open conflict, as happened in the case of the Greek Civil War. The battle for historical memory is essentially a battle about politics; however, the methods with which history is approached can reveal politics as a motivation to study history. By abandoning working class politics, in which historical memory was reproduced within organized struggle, the age of social movements usually entails diffused group and individualist approaches to memory. As such, postmemories can be tools through which history is enacted through memories ingrained in cultural practices and artefacts. Such postmemories are critical because they can also become part of creating the meaning of resistance, by increasing focus on the symbolic dimension of collective action

(Daphi & Zamponi, 2019, p. 400) and can be effective in building critical mass when engaging in contentious politics.

The Battle of Athens, Dekemvriana, was an event (very much associated with the Varkiza Treaty) with noteworthy impact both in terms of building a sense of national unity among the forces of the Greek state as well as international relations and political coalitions of that era (Vulliamy & Smith, 2014). Unofficially, it was thought of as the official start of the Greek Civil War, as the killing of many demonstrators showed the extent to which the state and its (mainly British) allies would allow any chance for delineating from the Western block. After the occupation, the influence of the Resistance movement, in which the National Liberation Front (EAM) had a leading role, backed by the Communist Party, was continually growing as its impact was extensively recognized (Vulliamy & Smith, 2014). Moreover, the logistics of creating such an army under the brutal occupation meant extensive nation-building skills on the part of the Resistance. This was in opposition to Britain's attempt to restore a political regime closer to its interests, which, though, was still in conflict with Germany's interests (Vulliamy & Smith, 2014).

Dekemvriana referred to the crowded demonstration of the 3rd of December 1944, when Britain, alongside local Nazi collaborators, opened fire against demonstrators and EAM members, sowing the seeds for the outbreak of the Civil War and the rise of the far-right in Greece (Vulliamy & Smith, 2014). Dekemvriana was followed by a period of White Terror (Panourgiá, 2009, pp. 78–80; Tsiras, 2011, p. 79) and the Civil War. During the so-called White Terror, was a period characterized by extreme policing and surveillance practices, while the National Guard (Ethnofylaki) (Panourgiá, 2009, p. 78) formed. That came as in opposition to the Red Terror, which referred to the Communist Peril. After the Varkiza Treaty and the disarmament of the left, the right-wing groups started forming the first political parties, which obtained a position in the parliament (Tsiras, 2011). While KKE was still banned, some of the most noteworthy far-right wing parties of that period were the Chi (X) Party and the National Political Union, which comprised smaller far-right groups and parties, as well as the National Rally, led by Papagos (Tsiras, 2011, p. 79). After the end of the Civil War, communism and the left were still considered as the enemy (Panourgiá, 2009; Tsiras, 2011), and that was reflected on the way that the political setting established after the Civil War, and for the decades to follow.

The Varkiza Treaty was considered a matter of an existential narrative for the political Greek left, as it became the vehicle by which the reconstructed Greek state used the truce to enforce and persecute the Resistance fighters

(Vlavianos, 1992). As the Greek Civil War and its aftermath has had a profound effect on the affinities, the programs, the stance, and narratives of political parties and other actors in Greek politics, Varkiza created a symbolic meaning regarding left politics and its connotation. Therefore, there is a variety of political actors which interpret the treaty as the rebirth of the state of Greece, following the liberation of Greece from German occupation, in World War II (WWII). The Varkiza Treaty has come to mean in popular culture of class actors and the popular strata the surrendering of arms, a sort of giving up on the part of the Democratic Army of Greece (DSE) on popular power (Vlavianos, 1992), subjecting the armed forces which liberated Greece under the bourgeois state, which was unable and unwilling to include the communists as has happened in other states (see, for example, the case of France, Italy). The Greek state has remained deeply anti-communist in rhetoric and stance, willing to openly fight for power and legitimization, utilizing foreign powers (primarily British initially, the United States later) to curb any resistance to its atrocious practices. In essence, the battle for the memory of Varkiza has come to debate whether the Treaty meant the abandonment of revolution (Iatrides, 2005) via military terms on the part of the working class and the popular strata.

VARKIZA TREATY ON YOUTUBE: METHODS, DATA, AND ANALYSIS

Digital and social media, and their affordances, prompted the emergence of new practices for social interaction and participation (Khan, 2017) in the public–private sphere. The internet, and especially YouTube, is perceived as being a source of ongoing, informal, and collaborative knowledge (Dubovi & Tabak, 2020). Knowledge construction is a process that starts with knowledge sharing and expands on "collective modification and examination of each other's ideas" (Dubovi & Tabak, 2020, p. 3), developing argumentative deliberation and thus knowledge building. YouTube is one of the most popular social media platforms that attracts diverse communities and users, providing a space for engagement and participation, whereas engagement includes aspects of both productive participation and consumption. Khan (2017, p. 239) suggests that comments, as user-generated content (UGC), have a significant contribution and impact on the way that individuals perceive reality and also contribute to the perception of the original content posted. In other words, YouTube is one of the primary platforms at this moment – situated within the context of dehistorization, revisionism, and the emergence of algorithmic identities – in time within which the politics and battle for memory take place. The impact that engagement and participation might have on the construction of collective memory regarding Civil War should be understood within the wider discussion regarding WWII and the processes of building memory and remembering, highlighting though the significant characteristics of the examined platform.

The data set was emerged by the collection of YouTube comments, posted after the video of the iconic scene of the Varkiza Treaty and the DSE surrendering of arms using the YouTube Data Tool (Rieder, 2015). The data collection was conducted focusing on the video with the highest number of views, after searching on YouTube the keywords "Varkiza Treaty." The "most viewed video" is one of the oldest uploaded in the platform and captures the very iconic scene of the Varkiza Treaty and the DSE surrendering of arms (popularity/views/date of post). The data set comprised 866 comments, produced by 381 unique users, as posted by the completion of data collection (25/02/21). After the collection of the data, these were inserted on Google spreadsheet and were analyzed focusing on the identification of key themes, as shaped by the public discussion and debates. Thematic Analysis here is used as an analytical method for the study of a range of research questions associated with people's experiences and the "representation and construction of particular phenomena in particular contexts" (Clarke & Braun, 2013, p. 121).

Thus, the analysis of the dataset concentrated on the identification of the main themes discussed, reflecting on questions around ideology, class, conflict, and historical continuities. In the first round of analysis, the data set which originally comprised 866 comments was narrowed down, by isolating the comments that didn't attract any interaction (likes or comments). Then, the 262 unique comments which were selected by the number of likes indicated viewpoints and arguments around which users participated in the public debate. In the next stage, the analysis looked at the discourses that situated in transnational, national, and the individual level.

The video in question is not as rare, in terms of content, as it was 11 years ago, when it was first posted. A similar or the same scene has been posted by several users during the past decade, on many occasions recognized as close to the KKE (for example, the well-known online zine *Atexnws*) or other random users. This is associated to the affordances of YouTube, as users who post can also manage the comments and thus the discussion after the video. At the same time, this reflects on a common practice of YouTube users to repost older videos in order to renew and maintain videos' online presence, in case previous published of the version of the content disappear online (unpublished).

The reproduction of a part of the video or the whole suggests that the content of the video is (a product) on demand. The examined video's duration is 4 minutes, and 59 seconds is a collage of video footage from archives of the channel of the parliament (Vouli TV) and of Greek documentaries. It starts by depicting the soldiers listening to their superior, presumably reading the Varkiza Treaty to them and subsequently the soldiers one by one returning their arms, amid tears. The scene is heightened by epic music, as if the soldiers are aware at that point of the historical significance of the event, contemplating on a defeat that was at that moment not known. Toward the very end of the video, a narrator explains that on December 12, 1945, the Varkiza Treaty was signed by EAM and the government. Then, an old female Resistance fighter admits that after that event "This was a terrible shock, we could not understand, why those won the war to surrender their weapons (referring to communist, anti-nazi partisans). We surrendered, crying. You are aware that then a persecution against the resistance fighters had begun." The narrator continued: "the Varkiza Treaty was a compromise under the light of certain conditions. EAM and KKE had indeed been defeated in Athens, but not in the rest of Greece, where ELAS had superiority in arms and fighters and controlled most of the territory of the country."

Overall, it could be considered that the video was not informative as the context was alluring toward the conditions in which the treaty was agreed. The video narrative guides the user toward the connotation of giving up on the means, to hold on power and win the war; it is affective in structure as it invites emotional responses in the comments section. Exploring the online discourse, the analysis focused on the identification of key debates occurred as observed in transnational, national, and individual level. These three streams point out the context in which the debates evolved and involved forces/actors.

Starting with the national context, users concentrated on the ideological division of the involved forces in WWII and then the Civil War (democratic forces and the far-right/Nazi groups). Here, the discussion concentrates mainly on the conflicted interests that the involved forces served, the Communist Party in contrast to far right/Nazi forces, as well as the historical continuities in the contemporary sociopolitical terrain (association to crisis politics and parties, worker rights, inequality, etc.). In this respect, there is a direct association among the working class, the labor movement and DSE, EAM-ELAS, and the way that these shaped contemporary national politics and were also shaped during the crisis. In this context, far-right/Nazi forces are understood as serving capitalist forces or as an outcome of contemporary capitalism – starting from WWII up to the financial crisis of 2008, and onward.

Another interesting finding in this stream is the references made to the "middle class" and the bourgeoise – what here is discussed as the so-called "political dynasties," in other words, the political families that rule the country. These are discussed in link to the subsequent developments of the decades to follow and were also associated to in contemporary politics (rise of far right and neo-Nazi groups/Golden Dawn and Fyssas, Syriza and the Communist Party, anarchist groups and class, etc.). In these debates, the contemporary left forces and the Communist parties are straightforwardly associated to the working class, while the bourgeoise are linked to the far-right politics, starting from Civil War up to what these represent nowadays.

In a transnational level, war and conflict are again discussed in terms of oppression and profit, escalating the existed debates from a national to a transnational level. Here, the main arguments as discussed in the previous stream are situated within the global political setting. Therefore, debates regarding WWII, Russia and Nazi Germany, Britain, the coalition with the United States, their contribution to Civil War, and their association to Greece, Greece as protectorate and imperialism, are some of the main schemes discussed, including questions over social justice, inequality, and class. Once again, the point of reference is the labor movement, class, and the conflicted interests of the bourgeoise.

On an individual level, or in a microlevel approach similar to the previous two, the debate is around the rise of far-right politics, as seen during WWII and then the evolution and association to contemporary politics, as these reflected on an individual level. Under the individual prism, most comments can be seen as, more than anything, being affective. In terms of agency, we cannot discern whether users engaged with the video as part of the platform's algorithmic curation or whether users searched for it. Users though engage to the platforms by both consuming the content in the form of the video and by producing content in the form of comments. In other examples, this supplementary process might also be associated to digitization of archive – an approach that we don't explore in this chapter. Regarding the UGC, not all users leave a comment, and when doing so, there is usually an affective element. Other affective affordances also contribute into this direction, such as the like and dislike button. Interestingly, the video has just 1,000 likes (out of 243 thousand views) but no dislikes. This is surprising given that comments under the video are mixed, in terms of reception.

Content wise, the discussions on an individual level ranged from complete personal stories to straightforward political inclinations. Many of them discussed their feelings toward the video, either against or in favor to the resistance fighters' tears that are depicted. The performative and affective elements of the video have awakened personal and family stories shared as well as other postmemories which the users have gathered from other mediums and procedures. These can be identified as micro-narratives of the personal sort, with affective engagements of users contributing both in favor and against the Resistance. Despite some of the comments attempting to connect with larger themes of historical continuities and truth, many remained within the limits and the path that the platform infrastructure and medium itself dictates (Smit et al., 2017).

THE GREEK CIVIL WAR, CULTURAL PRODUCTION, AND COLLECTIVE MEMORY

Kaisidou (2020) notes that the published novels during 2000–2015, which take as a central theme the Greek Civil War (1946–1949), were far outnumber those that were published between the years that followed the fall of the dictatorship (1967–1974). Thus, discussing this observation, the author notes that the generation of the early 21st century had no experiential connection to the events of the Greek Civil War but could rather build new ones, through mediated memories as constructed by previous generations. Given to the recent interest, there are various reasons that might have generated the reconsideration and discussion of the Greek Civil War. The process of understanding such historical events is in many cases an excuse to discuss political developments in the current era, by engaging in politics of memory (Lebow et al., 2006). As such, the intended transmitted memory from the previous generation is aimed not at uncovering some new shocking truth but as a discursive construct in an agonistic political terrain. Related to this is the attempt by what can be called broadly the right-wing political family to trivialize history, presenting and challenging an older slogan "hegemony of the left" (Boukala, 2021).

In this context, the left ostensibly assumed the victims' role after the Metapolitefsi period, attempting to use the fall of the military junta to push its political, economic, and social agenda. Under this light, the political violence which included both the Communist backed DSE (and ELAS) and the anti-communist state army with its allies was a game between two sides seeking power, and thus, violence is redeemed of the cause. At the same time, this serves also as a plane in which the political right can build on the "forgotten subjects" who here are branded as the victims of the communists. In many of the novels, the Greek Civil War acts as the terrain or the backdrop to the personal stories; an emphasis given to the personal drama minimizes the historical continuity, rejecting so-called grand narratives, which trivializes history by introducing personal fragmented temporalities. The methodological tool of such approaches was mostly oral history which enjoyed much interest and generated heated debates among scholars on history in postmodern times (Perks & Thomson, 2015). As such, the historical events become a cultural residue, upon which contemporary historical revisionism has been built. This, up to a point, is also evident to the debates around postmemories and affected memory, as seen in the analysis of data.

Of course, memory regarding historical events, and most indicatively coming from depictions and narratives of WWII, is not one-sided (Erll & Nünning, 2008; Misztal, 2003). The construction of memory usually serves national interests, and memorials are often reread and reconsidered in present time and under contemporary context/conditions and societies, with new meanings and signification continuously evolving (Erll & Nünning, 2008, p. 358). According to Zamponi (2020), collective memory is characterized by pluralism, particularly when viewed through the lens of social movements that use mediated memory and culture for political mobilization. Indeed, the construction of a common memory can be viewed as part of a tactical and cultural repertoire that can be used to forge solidarity among individual activists and social movements, in the absence of a unified grand narrative (Kubal & Becerra, 2014).

On many occasions, such memories can be partly constructed deliberately as part of a starting mythic story. The original idea from which the increasingly discipline of "memory studies" takes its reference point stems from Maurice Halbwachs and Lewis (1992) in the 1920s from which he understood memory to be a socially contingent action (Gensburger, 2016). What is remembered mostly comes from social practices such as religious and official or state memory mixing with familial memory passing through generations. As such, the combinations of stories can be varied according to where someone is born, the community which is raised and also the types of stories they have heard within the family. That means, different members of an imagined community (Anderson, 2006) may mean different things and interpret a historical event in different signs and symbolisms. In a similar way, this can also be understood focusing on ideology and the involved communities in online discourse.

Memory and remembering is understood as "becoming social" (Erll & Nünning, 2008, pp. 196–197), whereas individual and social remembering are still shaped by and, according to different contexts, steered by emotions and moral values (Erll & Nünning, 2008). Memory as being social is structured and maintained through the common sharing of events, symbols, and sociocultural contexts (Misztal, 2003, p. 11), while by extension, cultural memory is shared beyond historical discourse and is materialized through cultural means (2003, p. 12). Most importantly, the construction of memory presupposes collective – a group of people who identify with certain ideas, cultures, narratives, etc. – (Mena & Rintamäki, 2020) and social elements (Olick, 1999; Olick & Robbins, 1998) which the new digital environment undermines (Merrill et al., 2021). As also seen in the data analysis, digital media provide an additional layer on this process, with social and individual memory being possible to be negotiated, constructed, and argued in the digital space. Therefore, served interests, conflicted identities, and evolving perceptions of historical events and continuities are all contributing to shaping memory in the digital space – and beyond. That reflects questions around traditional debates regarding accessibility, participation, and further fragmentation on (social and collective) memory, as digital media features indicate.

The emphasis on studies of memory also coincides and expands with the demise of mass politics and "retreat from class" in theorizing and organizing social struggles (Wood, 1998) and the decoupling of historical events from a unified temporality (Jameson, 1991), as grand narratives of the modernist era have lost their appeal to multiple narratives that adhere to various temporalities, subsequently giving rise to a pastiche effect.

> *In the postmodern, then, the past itself has disappeared (along with the well-known "sense of the past" or historicity and collective memory).*

This could be perceived as an example of dehistoricization and Jameson (1991) suggests this is a necessary step in emptying events from context, in order to be more easily commercially consumed. If history makes sense in collective terms, memories, especially ones without attachment to history, make sense only in individual terms. It is an analogy to the political struggle of classes; the more history is disassembled into rhizomes, the more political subjects look more like individuals. In our data, debates pointing on ideology and historical continuities often are weakened due to the individual aspect (as seen in the examined stream). Therefore, memory, which may or may not be sourced from historical events, can be quite plastic in nature, with multiple functionalities as an empty signifier, without the ability to form a unified collective perception of history. A triumph of memory – personal, fallible, fragmented, and ahistorical – over history, which is a collective social and political process.

Skalidakis (2015) reflects on a revisionist interpretation that actively seeks to portray the Resistance forces during the Occupation period as violent villains. This perspective raises questions about their role and allegiance, particularly as those same liberation forces later participated in the Greek Civil War. While the Resistance forces in other countries fighting an anti-fascist war were included in the postwar period, at least to some extent, as they had no intention of returning to the previous status quo. In Greece, there was no such case of collaborative spirit or even tolerance from the bourgeois class nor from the elites or the Allies (the British mainly), as they sought to eliminate the extensive power and influence the forces of Resistance managed to create, especially outside Athens.

Skalidakis (2015) suggests that the economics of the matter are a serious area of understudy, which not only can shed more light into the actual events but can also explain the decisions made by actors during the development of the Greek Civil War. An indicative example was the use and control of humanitarian aid (mainly by the United States) that was supplied via the International Red Cross and distributed through channels controlled by remaining and reorganizing bourgeois forces, with the intent of luring areas and population that were collaborating or were allegiance to the Resistance forces. Looking at the battlefield of the Greek Civil War after the Second World War, the areas which did not benefit from the humanitarian aid were evidently Resistance bastions, that would form the basis of a parallel network authorities (Kivernisi tou Vounou) and institutions for survival and thus challenge the legitimacy of a fragile bourgeois state.

This is a major difference to historical revisionist voices: whereas historians such as Skalidakis (2015) try to find materialist explanations and embark on historical projects which require temporal continuity, other historians and scholars attempt at creating and contextualize a number of other narratives which may or may not require temporal continuity. Fragmentation, personalization via cherry picking (the sorts of YouTube video in this case), and alternative temporalities of historical narratives are the techniques that contribute to this type of historiography as it seems to suffer the most from the post-memory of the Greek Civil War. In this sense, historical revisionism is directly linked to an attempt to naturalize the existing order; this is how historical events are utilized for present-day political maneuvering. Micro-narratives and storytelling methods help articulate the past without the essence of historical process; it is negation of the very essence of collective class struggles through negating the basis for analyzing them. On top of this process, which requires institutional support (e.g., the Greek state, the German embassy, etc.) rests a commercial technical assemblage of algorithms and actors on the internet, which works as an extra layer of obfuscation, not necessarily promoting a particular narrative but nonetheless amplifying the randomization of history (as technique reconstructing past events, thus affecting collective memory). Individuated subjects (subjects that are dissected and categorized based on commercial interests as audiences) are presented and recommended to historical videos of the events based on the commercialized data of the user profile. Hence, the video might have appeared to users according to the information cookies and tracking software, between commercials and other unrelated videos. Fragmentation and randomization of history is hardly a Greek phenomenon, but rather a general tendency in producing history that can be traced to the retreat from class politics and historical materialism, and the cultural turn in historiography (Stone, 1979). Therefore, while it has a long tradition, digital media further reinforced such procedures, through the emerge of new outputs which make history more fluid and flexible.

CONCLUSION

Digital platforms provided new opportunities for the dissemination of historical information, but they also indicated significant challenges. The ease of creating and sharing digital content means that historical narratives are reproduced, within platform affordances and limitations, and as another flow of information, these can be manipulated, distorted, or misrepresented. Digital media provided an alternative space for the rapid spread of alternative histories, via a bottom-up dynamic process, and had a significant impact on reception of histories and the proliferation of revisionist narratives. Histories produced digitally can also be subject to revisionism. Historical revisionism refers to the modification or rejection of historic narratives, often based on the interpretation, selection, or availability of archives, as well as the recovery of new historical information.

Jameson (1991) notes that the cultural logic of late capitalism erodes historical consciousness and reduces memory to a commodity, which can be bought and sold. In this context, the digitization of archive facilitates the manipulation and distortion of historical content and promotes mis/disinformation (via users' engagement and so on). This is also associated to fragmentation and decontextualization of history, promoting a superficial and ahistorical understanding of the past, easily manipulated and distorted for political or commercial purposes. The ease of digital manipulation contributes to the spread of misinformation and conspiracy theories, which can further erode historical consciousness and critical thinking.

Looking into postmemories, history and historical events are turned into trauma stories (instead of political), which negate the possibility of history in the modernist sense. The exclusion of the hard evidence of the Greek Civil War becomes mere memories of trauma about the defeat of the democratic army, the mistakes of the leadership of the Communist Party, and the subsequent misery of missed chances to build an alternative future. Hirsch (2008) notes that "the bodily, psychic, and affective impact of trauma and its aftermath, the ways in which one trauma can recall, or reactivate, the effects of another, exceed the bounds of traditional historical archives and methodologies." The postmemories of the Greek Civil War therefore are not about reflecting but mainly about processing the trauma of losing the chance for an alternative world, coping with the defeat and strengthening the narratives of There Is No Alternative (TINA) of 21st century perpetual memorandum times, the ever-growing list of anti-popular programs. It is in a sense learning to live with a perpetual defeat.

Thus, the post-memory artefacts that are available on commercial platforms feeding on the value of user engagement such as YouTube do not constitute just another way of learning and discussing history in public. They are affective machines with the appearance of reflective public discourse, which lack the capacity to articulate historical discussions. As such, even when discussions transverse class and agonistic politics, against deliberation and consensus, the temporal and dividual fragmentation of history into memories amplify the message of organized attempts at historical revisionism of earlier mediums such as novels and cinema. As the Greek Civil War proves to be a mere backdrop to personal drama in the aforementioned mediums, the YouTube video provides the post-memory of Greek Civil War as an excuse for user engagement in a private setting (the laptop, the house, etc.). Reflecting upon this, it would then seem as natural development in assessing such videos and the filter bubbles they welcome as part of the class struggle (in micro/meso/macro level) against collective memory, against history as a scientific discipline and epistemology, and ultimately against organized politics of the working class.

The democratization of historical content on platforms like YouTube may appear to signal an empowering spread of historical knowledge to the masses. However, when viewed through the lens of "platformization" of memory and development of commercial infrastructure for the digital mediation of memories (Smit et al., 2024), this democratization can be seen, in fact, also as a guise for the relentless commodification of history produced as spectacle. In addition, this process produces private temporalities within which history as spectacle is consumed, enhancing affective elements rather than materialist conceptions of history. The means of historical production and dissemination, now ostensibly accessible to all, serves a free market infrastructural system that thrives on the marketization of information.

Within such seemingly democratized landscape of historical videos, the Marxist concept of real subsumption becomes evident (O'Connell, 2019). We could thus argue of "real subsumption of memory under capital" to attempt and expanding the literature in explaining the ways in which capitalist modes of cultural production (whether professional or hobbyist) have transformed the relationship between memory and the ability to read history not as consumable bites of simulacra. In this context, memory can no longer be seen as a cultural or social resource, but rather as a commodity that can be bought and sold in the marketplace, just as the marketplace of ideas. This transformation has significant implications for the way in which history is produced, consumed, and understood. The digital platform, understood in much of literature as expanded public sphere, can be seen as an increasingly commodified space for the dissemination of history, which inevitably succumb to the logic of cultural production under capitalism and thus reproduces postmodern subjectivities. The videos, in their attempt to appeal to a wide audience, risk becoming simulacra – hyperreal representations that prioritize entertainment over historical accuracy. The democratization process, then, paradoxically leads to the proliferation of historical simulacra divorced from the material realities of the past.

REFERENCES

Alvanos, R. (2022). *The Greek civil war: Memories in war and contemporary political identities* [Ο Ελληνικός Εμφύλιος: Μνήμες Σε Πόλεμο Και Σύγχρονες Πολίτικες Ταυτότητες, in greek]. Epikentro.

Anderson, B. (2006). *Imagined communities: Reflections on the origin and spread of nationalism*. Verso.

Boukala, S. (2021). We need to talk about the hegemony of the left: The normalisation of extreme right discourse in Greece. *Journal of Language and Politics*, 361–382. https://doi.org/10.1075/jlp.19053.bou

Boyd, D. (2010). Social network sites as networked publics: Affordances, dynamics, and implications. In *A networked self* (pp. 47–66). Routledge.

Carbajal, I. A., & Caswell, M. (2021). Critical digital archives: A review from archival studies. *The American Historical Review*, *126*(3), 1102–1120.

Challenor, J., & Ma, M. (2019). A review of augmented reality applications for history education and heritage visualisation. *Multimodal Technologies and Interaction*, *3*(2), 39.

Christin, A. (2020). The ethnographer and the algorithm: Beyond the black box. *Theory and Society*, *49*(5–6). 897–918. https://doi.org/10.1007/s11186-020-09411-3

Clarke, V., & Braun, V. (2013). Teaching thematic analysis: Overcoming challenges and developing strategies for effective learning. *The Psychologist*, *26*(2). 120–123.

Danforth, L. M., & Van Boeschoten, R. (2019). *Children of the Greek civil war: Refugees and the politics of memory*. University of Chicago Press.

Daphi, P., & Zamponi, L. (2019). Exploring the movement-memory nexus: Insights and ways forward. *Mobilization: An International Quarterly*, *24*(4), 399–417. https://doi.org/10.17813/1086-671x-24-4-399

Dubovi, I., & Tabak, I. (2020). An empirical analysis of knowledge co-construction in YouTube comments. *Computers & Education*, *156*, 103939. https://doi.org/10.1016/j.compedu.2020.103939

Erll, A., & Nünning, A. A. (Eds.). (2008). *Cultural memory studies: An international and interdisciplinary handbook*. Walter de Gruyter.

Fritsch, M. (2006). *The promise of memory: History and politics in Marx, Benjamin, and Derrida*. SUNY Press.

Funkenstein, A. (1989). Collective memory and historical consciousness. *History & Memory*, *1*(1), 5–26.

Gensburger, S. (2016). Halbwachs' studies in collective memory: A founding text for contemporary 'memory studies'? *Journal of Classical Sociology*, 396–413. https://doi.org/10.1177/1468795X16656268

Gillespie, T. (2014). The relevance of algorithms. *Media Technologies*, 167–194. https://doi.org/10.7551/mitpress/9780262525374.003.0009

Gitelman, L., & Jackson, V. (2013). Introduction. In L. Gitelman (Ed.), *"Raw data" is an oxymoron*. MIT Press.

Gkotzaridis, E. (2011). What is behind the concept: Fragmentation and internal critique in the revisionist debates of Greece and Ireland. In *What is behind the concept: Fragmentation and internal critique in the revisionist debates of Greece and Ireland* (pp. 87–110).

Goriunova, O. (2019). The digital subject: People as data as persons. *Theory, Culture & Society, 36*(6), 125–145.

Hadjivassiliou, V. (2018). *The movement of the pendulum: The individual and society in modern Greek prose: 1974–2017*. Polis.

Halbwachs, M., & Lewis, A. C. (1992). *On collective memory*. University of Chicago Press.

Hansen-Glucklich, J. (2014). *Holocaust memory reframed: Museums and the challenges of representation*. Rutgers University Press.

Hirsch, M. (2008). The generation of postmemory. *Poetics Today, 29*(1). 103–128. https://doi.org/10.1215/03335372-2007-019

Hirsch, M. (2012). *The generation of postmemory: Writing and visual culture after the holocaust*. Columbia University Press.

Hoskins, A. (2009). Digital network memory. In A. Erll & A. Rigney (Eds.), *Mediation, remediation, and the dynamics of cultural memory* (pp. 91–106). Series: Media and cultural memory (6). Walter de Gruyter. ISBN 9783110204445.

Hoskins, A. (Ed.). (2018). *Digital memory studies: Media pasts in transition*. Routledge.

Iatrides, J. O. (2005). Revolution or self-defense? Communist goals, strategy, and tactics in the Greek civil war. *Journal of Cold War Studies, 7*(3), 3–33.

Jameson, F. (1991). *Postmodernism or the cultural logic of late capitalism*. Duke University Press.

Jameson, F. (2015). *The ancients and the postmoderns: On the historicity of forms*. Verso Books.

Kaisidou, V. (2020). The novel of the Greek civil war in the twenty-first century: (Post)memory and the weight of the past. In *Byzantine and modern Greek studies* (Vol. 44, pp. 301–318). Tome.

Khan, M. L. (2017). Social media engagement: What motivates user participation and consumption on YouTube? *Computers in Human Behavior*, 236–247. https://doi.org/10.1016/j.chb.2016.09.024

Kubal, T., & Becerra, R. (2014). Social movements and collective memory. *Sociology Compass*, 865–875. https://doi.org/10.1111/soc4.12166

Lebow, R. N., Kansteiner, W., & Fogu, C. (2006). *The politics of memory in postwar Europe*. Duke University Press.

Lippmann, R. P. (1997). Speech recognition by machines and humans. *Speech Communication*, 22(1), 1–15.

Livingstone, S. (2005). On the relation between audiences and publics. In S. Livingstone (Ed.), *Audiences and publics: When cultural engagement matters for the public sphere. Changing media – Changing Europe series* (Vol. 2, pp. 17–41). Intellect Books.

Locatelli, E. (2021). Towards the platformization of (social) media memory: Articulating archive, assemblage, and ephemerality. In *Comunicazioni sociali: Journal of media, performing arts and cultural studies: Nuova serie: XLIII, 1* (pp. 162–173). Vita e Pensiero. 1827-7969 – Casalini id: 4844642.

Lukacs, J. (2017). *Historical consciousness: The remembered past*. Routledge.

MacKenzie, I., & Porter, R. (2019). Totalizing institutions critique and resistance. *Contemporary Political Theory*, 233–249. https://doi.org/10.1057/s41296-019-00336-w

Makhortykh, M., Urman, A., & Ulloa, R. (2021). Hey Google is it what the holocaust looked like? Auditing algorithmic curation of visual historical content on web search engines. *First Monday*. https://doi.org/10.5210/fm.v26i10.11562

Marantzidēs, N. A. (2023). *Under Stalin's shadow : A global history of Greek communism*. Northern Illinois University Press an imprint of Cornell University Press.

Marantzidis, N. (2013). The Greek civil war (1944–1949) and the international communist system. *Journal of Cold War Studies*, 25–54.

McKelvey, F. (2014). Algorithmic media need democratic methods: Why publics matter. *Canadian Journal of Communication*, 39(4), 597–613.

Mena, S., & Rintamäki, J. (2020). Managing the past responsibly: A collective memory perspective on responsibility, sustainability and ethics. In O. Laasch, R. Suddaby, R. E. Freeman, & D. Jamali (Eds.), *Research handbook of responsible management* (pp. 470–483). Edward Elgar Publishing.

Merrill, S., Keightley, E., & Daphi, P. (2021). *Social movements cultural memory and digital media: Mobilising mediated remembrance*. Palgrave Macmillan.

Misztal, B. A. (2003). *Theories of social remembering*. Open University Press.

Navickas, K. (2018). A return to materialism? Putting social history back into place. In *New directions in cultural and social history*. Bloomsbury Academic.

O'Sullivan, D. (2011). What is an Encyclopedia. From Pliny to Wikipedia. In *Lovink Geert Nathaniel Tkacz and Institute of network cultures (Amsterdam Netherlands). Critical point of view: A Wikipedia reader* (pp. 34–50). Institute of Network Cultures.

O'Connell, H. C. (2019). Marxism. In *The Routledge companion to cyberpunk culture* (pp. 282–290). Routledge.

Olick, J. K. (1999). Collective memory: The two cultures. *Sociological Theory*, 333–348.

Olick, J. K., & Robbins, J. (1998). Social memory studies: From 'collective memory' to the historical sociology of mnemonic practices. *Annual Review of Sociology*, 105–140.

Pangrazio, L., & Selwyn, N. (2023). *Critical data literacies: Rethinking data and everyday life*. The MIT Press.

Panourgiá, N. (2009). *Dangerous citizens: The Greek left and the terror of the state* (1st ed.). Fordham University Press.

Pariser, E. (2014). *The filter bubble: How the new personalized web is changing what we read and how we think*. Penguin Books.

Perks, R., & Thomson, A. (2015). *The oral history reader*. Routledge/Taylor & Francis Group. http://site.ebrary.com/id/11127832

Rieder, B. (2015). YouTube data tools (version 1.31). [Software]. https://tools.digitalmethods.net/netvizz/youtube/

Schneider, F. (2018). Mediated massacre: Digital nationalism and history discourse on China's web. *Journal of Asian Studies*, 429–452. https://doi.org/10.1017/S0021911817001346

Skalidakis, Y. (2015). From resistance to counterstate: The making of revolutionary power in the liberated zones of occupied Greece 1943-1944. *Journal of Modern Greek Studies*, 155–184.

Smit, R., Heinrich, A., & Broersma, M. (2017). Witnessing in the new memory ecology: Memory construction of the Syrian conflict on YouTube. *New Media & Society*, 19(2), 289–307.

Smit, R., Jacobsen, B., & Annabell, T. (2024). The multiplicities of platformed remembering. *Memory, Mind & Media*, 3, e3.

Stone, L. (1979). The revival of narrative: Reflections on a new old history. *Past & Present*, N85(19791101), 3–24.

Tsiras, E. (2011). *The new far right in Greece: Organizational evolution, electoral influence and political speech of the People's Orthodox Rally (LAOS)* [Διατριβή: Η νέα άκρα δεξιά στην Ελλάδα: οργανωτική εξέλιξη, εκλογική επιρροή και πολιτικός λόγος του Λαϊκού Ορθόδοξου Συναγερμού]. Ph.D. University of Macedonia. National Archive of Ph.D. Theses, Thesis.ekt.gr. http://thesis.ekt.gr/thesisBookReader/id/28119#page/1/mode/2up. Accessed on March 31, 2017.

Van Dijck, J. (2007). *Mediated memories in the digital age*. Stanford University Press.

Vecchione, B., Levy, K., & Barocas, S. (2021). Algorithmic auditing and social justice: Lessons from the history of audit studies. In *Equity and access in algorithms, mechanisms, and optimization*. [Preprint]. https://doi.org./10.1145/3465416.3483294

Vlavianos, H. (1992). The Greek communist party: Resistance or revolution? In *Greece, 1941–49: From resistance to civil war*. St Antony's. Palgrave Macmillan. https://doi.org/10.1007/978-1-349-21857-8_2

Vulliamy, E., & Smith, H. (2014, November 30). Athens 1944: Britain's dirty secret. *The Guardian.* https://www.theguardian.com/world/2014/nov/30/athens-1944-britains-dirty-secret

Wood, E. M. (1998). *The retreat from class: A new "true" socialism* (Rev. ed.). Verso.

Zamponi, L. (2020). #ioricordo, beyond the Genoa G8: Social practices of memory work and the digital remembrance of contentious pasts in Italy. In S. Merrill, E. Keightley, & P. Daphi (Eds.), *Social movements, cultural memory and digital media: Mobilising mediated remembrance* (pp. 141–171). Palgrave Macmillan.